THE LAST JUDGEMENT
BY ANTHONY CARO

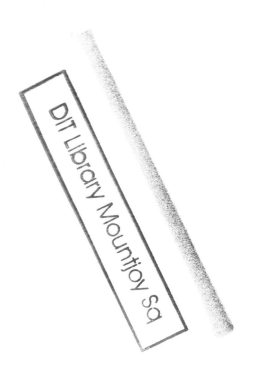

48.
esposizione
internazionale
d'arte

▼ MUSEUM **WÜRTH**

With the generous support of
the Würth Group

THE LAST JUDGEMENT
BY ANTHONY CARO

WITH CONTRIBUTIONS BY
PETER BAELZ, HANS MAGNUS ENZENSBERGER, NADINE GORDIMER,
ROBERT HINDE, PHILIP RYLANDS, JOHN SPURLING
AND PHOTOGRAPHS BY DAVID BUCKLAND

PUBLISHED BY VERLAG PAUL SWIRIDOFF

CONTENTS

FOREWORD
REINHOLD WÜRTH

For me, and for many others, the most important British sculptor since Henry Moore is Sir Anthony Caro. Several of his works are in the collection of the Museum Würth, the first having been acquired in 1995.

Today, Caro's sculpture is world famous and needs no further endorsement – especially not from a layman like me. However, I am again and again impressed how powerfully and directly the artist uses steel, stoneware and other materials, whilst at the same time imbuing his sculptures with a sense of lightness.

I met Anthony Caro for the first time in 1996 and we immediately took a great liking to each other. Time and again my observation about famous artists I have met was also true with Anthony Caro: modest, ingenious, charming and above all friendly with a sense of fun.

When I addressed him as Sir Anthony, in accordance with his title, he remarked that this honorary title is very nice and well meant, but that it is especially useful when making a reservation in a restaurant - for often he then gets a table at the window. So his good humour is not only written on his face and shows in his personality, but also in the character of his sculpture.

In 1998, together with my wife and the head of the museum, C. Sylvia Weber, I had the chance to visit Anthony Caro in his London studio, where he was busy working on parts of his "Last Judgement" sculpture. I was immediately intrigued. After having seen the model of the whole installation that he intended, I was moved and enthusiastic about the ambition, depth and scope of this work.

"The Last Judgement" will be shown to the public for the first time as part of the 1999 Venice Biennale. Without doubt it is one of the most important sculptures Anthony Caro has made: for in addition to its fine details, it expresses, with its challenging three-dimensionality, a depth of artistic creation that goes beyond the religious subject matter and will remain valid for all time.

Due to the current conflict in Kosovo – only a few flight minutes away from Venice – Caro's work has gained a dimension none of us could have foreseen. If there will ever be a Last Judgement or Divine Justice, these crimes will never be forgotten.

A work of art like this can only be created by a man who can rise above the present and is able to dedicate his art to the whole of mankind without regard to race, religion or culture. To be honest, I am more than a little proud that it was possible to secure this great masterpiece of Sir Anthony Caro's for the Museum Würth.

PREFACE
ANTHONY CARO

The *Last Judgement* may seem different in character from most of my earlier sculpture, but the same sensibility is at work. Its rhythms are similar, it is a piece one walks through, the works reveal themselves from close up. Unlike most of my work which is a celebration of life through the language of sculpture, the *Last Judgement* makes a comment on social and political behaviour. Europe's history is thick with horrors. My *Last Judgement* is a response to present day atrocities, although at the end it holds out some hope of a brighter future.

Unlike the *Trojan War* an earlier group which grew out of my immediate contact with ceramic clay, the idea of making a Last Judgement had been fermenting in my mind before I began the series. The stoneware parts were made in the ceramic studio of Hans Spinner in Grasse in 1996. I owe Hans a great deal: not only because of his feeling for the material and craft but also because of his perfect empathy with my intentions. After firing in the wood kiln the clay units were sent to London; in my studio there I slowly developed them into sculptures. I added steel and jarrah wood (old railway sleepers) as well as a few parts of oak and of concrete. Almost all the groups are set in boxes much as each wall painting in Giotto's chapel in Padua or in Assisi sits within a similar frame.

The sculpture cannot be fully appreciated in what might be called 'art' terms. Most of my art can: this is why I've sometimes been called an 'artist's artist'. There's no right or wrong in this, the art is no more nor less human - it's simply whether the humanity comes through one channel or another.

Because of the social and political implications I decided in this publication to invite authors to explore themes which are relevant to the subject matter or focus on the issues raised. To place the work in the setting of its historical lineage I asked Philip Rylands, whose speciality is Renaissance art, to make a survey of expressions of the Last Judgement and the Apocalypse in the art of the past. Nadine Gordimer has lived in South Africa during and since apartheid and her novels deal with personal themes within that setting; she writes about the creative artist; working in the political arena. Hans Magnus Enzensberger gives his poetic interpretation of themes underlying the Last Judgement and his two poems written and translated especially for the catalogue reflect my own feelings. Robert Hinde writes about human violence from the scientist's standpoint; a world authority on animal behaviour he has extended his studies to include human activity. Peter Baelz has for a long time interested himself in how the pursuit of art mirrors that of morality; he discusses how in each we strive for 'the good' without knowing quite what it is. John Spurling's introduction and quotations clarify the subject matter of the episodes which make up my *Last Judgement*. His texts drawn from a wide variety of sources seem to underline the consistency of human behaviour and endeavour throughout history.

Each of these busy and distinguished people agreed without hesitation to contribute to this unusual project. I am most grateful to them for the time and effort they have given to it.

Without the generous sponsorship of Dr. h. c. Reinhold Würth and the wholehearted support of his museum's director Sylvia Weber, this sculpture would not have seen the light of day. Reinhold Würth has a real passion for art. He has a museum with changing exhibitions within his headquarters so that modern and contemporary art can be enjoyed by everyone who works there, and to house his collection he is now building a new museum in Schwäbisch Hall. His enthusiasm on first seeing the *Last Judgement* in my studio gave me great encouragement.

My special thanks go to Ian Barker who with the endorsement of Annely and David Juda has seen the development of the sculpture at every stage and helped overcome many practical problems; he made many visits to my studio and to Venice and with steady and characteristic efficiency organised the smooth running of the exhibition.

My thanks to the Peggy Guggenheim Collection in Venice and to the British Council who have given their warm support to the show, and to Harald Szeeman and Agnes Kohlmeyer of the Venice Biennale who facilitated the selection of a suitable exhibition venue.

I would like to thank David Buckland for his photographs of the works and Kate Stephens for her catalogue design. Both of these artists have worked with me before and both have understood and entered into the spirit of the sculpture.

My special thanks go to the team of helpers in and out of my studio who fabricated all the parts of the sculpture; working long hours and carrying out the many changes needed as the work grew, Patrick Cunningham, Gavin Morris, Tim Peacock, Beth Cullen, Mike Bolus, Doug Burton, Andy Owens and Tina Gallifent. Also I am grateful to Jo Oliver and Tristan King, Jana Fowler, Gary Doherty, Dave Williams, Stephen Manual, Christoph Bueble, Chiara Barbieri and Beate Barner, Tonia Moulton, Laura Henderson and Beatrice Behlen all of whom have, in one way or another, assisted greatly on the project.

My sons Tim and Paul each brought fresh and useful responses to the project. Above all I want to thank my wife Sheila, whose eye and whose counsel I have depended on all my life, and whose generosity and patience for three years as the *Last Judgement* invaded our lives, is unbounded.

THE LAST JUDGEMENT BY ANTHONY CARO
AT THE VENICE BIENNALE 1999

Day of Judgment? It is a synonym for the present moment – it is eternally going on. It is not so much as a moment – it is just the line that has no breadth between past and future. There is not – cannot be, if you think it out – any other Day of Judgment.

Sir Edward Burne-Jones in conversation with Dr Sebastian Evans, 1893, quoted in *Memorials of Edward Burne-Jones*

Surely though we place Hell under earth, the Devil's walk and purlue is about it; men speake too popularly who place it in those flaming mountaines, which to grosser apprehensions represent Hell. The heart of man is the place the devill dwels in.

Thomas Browne, *Religio Medici*

THE LAST JUDGEMENT
AT THE ANTICHI GRANAI, VENICE BIENNALE 1999

All works were completed between 1995 and 1999.
Materials used include stoneware, concrete, oak,
jarrah wood, ekki wood, brass and steel.

THE BELL TOWER 384 x 617 x 122 cm
THE DOOR OF DEATH 222 x 193 x 71 cm
CHARON 208 x 123 x 101.5 cm
HELL IS A CITY 208.5 x 120 x 80 cm
WITHOUT MERCY 219 x 126 x 86 cm
UNKNOWN SOLDIER 208 x 123 x 90 cm
SHADES OF NIGHT 218 x 386 x 117 cm
ELYSIAN FIELDS 210 x 164 x 87.5 cm
TERESIAS 209 x 120 x 93 cm
TORTURE BOX 208.5 x 110.5 x 95 cm
STILL LIFE SKULLS 155 x 111 x 152 cm
FLESH 209 x 118 x 74 cm
GREED AND ENVY 210 x 111 x 90 cm
SACRIFICE 126 x 150 x 109 cm
SALOMÉ DANCES 211 x 104 x 169 cm
PRISONERS 205 x 202 x 82.5 cm
CONFESSION 206 x 113 x 64 cm
CIVIL WAR 206 x 375 x 104 cm
JUDAS 207 x 118 x 71 cm
TRIBUNAL 224 x 218.5 x 137 cm
POISON CHAMBER 209.5 x 118 x 78.5 cm
THE FURIES 208.5 x 126 x 95 cm
JACOB'S LADDER 211 x 139.5 x 84.5 cm
THE FURIES 208.5 x 126 x 95 cm
THE LAST TRUMP
· 223.5 x 70 x 201 cm
· 183 x 63.5 x 170 cm
· 214 x 68.5 x 175 cm
· 228.5 x 71.5 x 186 cm
GATE OF HEAVEN 237.5 x 185.5 x 69 cm

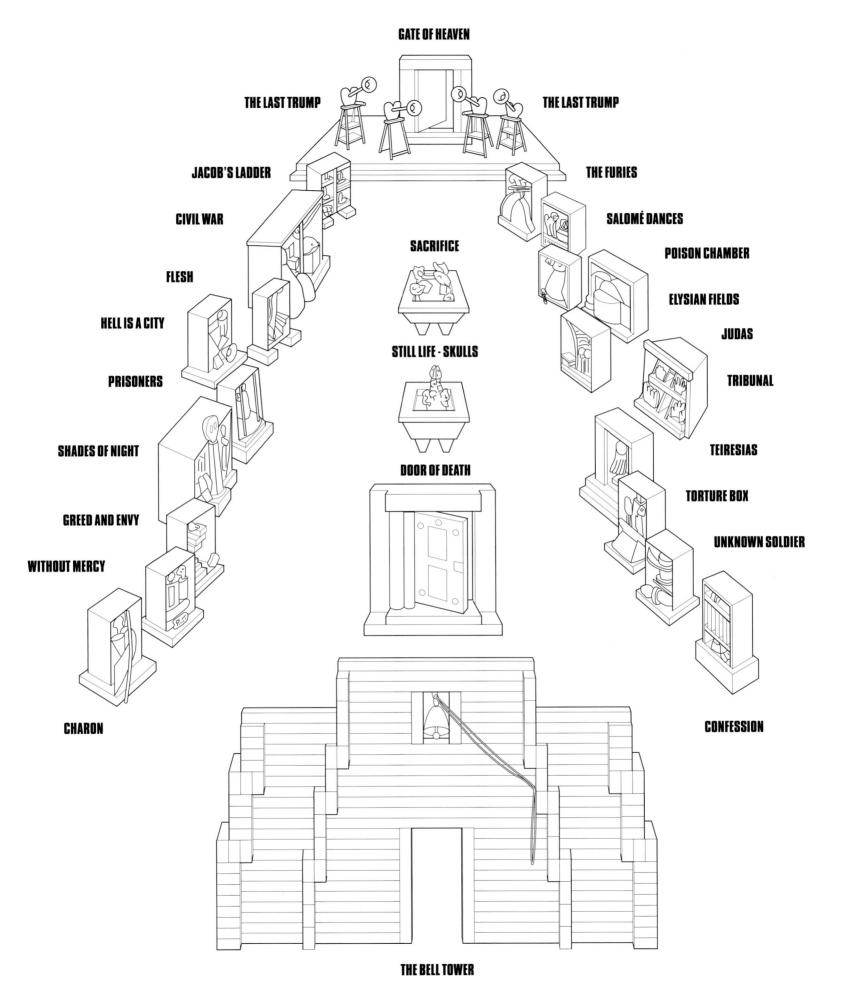

GATE OF HEAVEN

THE LAST TRUMP

THE LAST TRUMP

JACOB'S LADDER

THE FURIES

CIVIL WAR

SALOMÉ DANCES

SACRIFICE

POISON CHAMBER

FLESH

ELYSIAN FIELDS

HELL IS A CITY

JUDAS

STILL LIFE - SKULLS

PRISONERS

TRIBUNAL

SHADES OF NIGHT

TEIRESIAS

DOOR OF DEATH

GREED AND ENVY

TORTURE BOX

WITHOUT MERCY

UNKNOWN SOLDIER

CHARON

CONFESSION

THE BELL TOWER

ENTRANCE

VIOLENCE BETWEEN INDIVIDUALS, GROUPS AND STATES
ROBERT HINDE

22 Three extracts from a day's newspaper:

"US F-15E's dropped more than 30, 2,000 lb
and 500 lb laser guided bombs"

"....five people were killed after a mob of Christians burnt
Muslim homes and threw petrol bombs at worshippers
emerging from a mosque..."

"One tourist and two Ugandans were killed as the raiders,
wearing camouflage and carrying automatic rifles, burst
into the sites."

IT sometimes seems as though violence is ubiquitous. Every day the newspapers bring more reports of murders, of inter-group conflicts, of wars, of genocide. The suffering that violence brings to the victims, the irreplaceable loss suffered by relatives, the dehumanisation of the perpetrators, too easily become everyday matters. We accept them because they seem to be there all the time, and because the reports we read lack the blood and guts of suffering, because the horrors are sanitised. Yet, the world does not have to be like that. And if we accept that things can be different, we can move on to search for ways to make them so.

And there is hope, for violence is not an inevitable consequence of being human. Violent actions are conspicuous: they hit the headlines while countless acts of selflessness, kindness, consideration for others, go unremarked. Individuals have the capacity to behave with compassion as well as with violence. We must therefore ask, what are the forces that, on occasion, dominate the better aspects of human nature and allow aggressiveness to come to the surface?

Let us start early in development. Newborns have the potential to develop into loving, caring, cooperative adults, or to become assertive, egocentric, and selfish, or, as with most of us, something in between. In the course of development individual differences are determined by multiple interacting factors. Genetic differences probably play a role: certainly men are more prone to show physical violence, though women can hold their own in verbal aggression. More important are experiential issues: we now know a good deal about what determines the balance between the two extremes. In very broad terms, in the first few years of life loving care, coupled with sensitive firm control, swings the balance towards cooperativeness; harsh control with physical punishment, or else indulgent lack of control, towards selfishness. Punishment for aggressive acts is likely to be counter-productive: the child may learn that its behaviour has undesirable consequences, but the pain suffered tends to induce aggression directed elsewhere, and the aggression displayed by the punisher implies that violence is acceptable. Of course, the suggestion that there are two possible extreme routes for development, one involving cooperation for the common good and the other leading towards self-seeking and aggressiveness, is a gross simplification, for humans are both more complicated and more diverse than that implies. However, it is a useful approximation for present purposes, for it emphasises that understanding the bases of violence requires us to ask how the balance between prosocial and antisocial behaviour becomes shifted towards the latter pole, and that we all have the potential for both.

Why should human development be like this? After all, it could be that harsh and relentless punishment for wrong doing would lead to children becoming more sensitive to right and wrong. Here we can only speculate, but one possibility comes from the fact that human nature has been shaped by the operation of natural selection on the continuing interaction between the genes that give us the capacity for humanity and the world we experience. The genes have changed little in the last fifty thousand years, so that our basic psychological potentialities remain little changed from those with which natural selection endowed our ancestors. They too had potentialities for kindness and cooperation as well as self-serving violence. We can speculate that in some environments aggressive assertiveness paid off, in others the benefits of group living put a premium on cooperation. The best predictor of the environment to be encountered in adulthood was that encountered in childhood. So perhaps natural selection has acted to link the experiences of childhood to behaviour appropriate for the circumstances of adulthood. While a harsh environment led to strict parenting, and the children grew up to have assertive characteristics suited to such an environment, a benign environment had the opposite effects, favouring benign parenting and children disposed to be more cooperative. Again, of course, the dichotomy is deceptive, and natural selection presumably acted to fine-tune development to probable later experience.

Of course, experiences in early childhood are not indelible. Later, other factors enter - peer pressure, the example of respected others, media influence, and so on. Given the multiplicity of factors affecting personality, it is to be expected that most people are neither pure saints nor unredeemable sinners, but can behave selfishly or unselfishly according to circumstances. What then causes some individuals, sometimes, to swing into violence? Here it is critically important to recognise that the bases of violence differ according to the level of social complexity with which one is concerned. We may consider three cases, recognising that they lie on a continuous spectrum - first violence between individuals, and then violence between small groups, and finally large-scale international war.

Some children, though very few, are teasers: they seem to enjoy hurting others and delight in the pain of their victims. Perhaps some adults are similar. And some aggressive acts result from the orders of authority figures. But for the most part the perpetrators of aggressive acts are seldom single-minded, aggression being a means to an end. Most often, aggression is accompanied by acquisitiveness, assertiveness, or fear. Even the teasers may be motivated by a sort of assertiveness, needing to improve their self-image. But the important issue is that the incidence of violence would be less in a world where needs were satisfied, where people were content with their self-image, where they had no need to fear. Where individuals see themselves in danger of being exploited they tend to cultivate an image of toughness and irritability, as in many modern cities. This is exacerbated by lack of employment, and by capitalist materialism and competitiveness. Violence also tends to be more frequent where there are large income differences between rich and poor, and where the physical situation or mobility of individuals decreases the feeling of community. Perhaps all these issues can be seen as contributing to feelings of frustration and alienation.

Individuals differ in their propensity for aggression. Not only are boys on average more physically aggressive than girls, but their propensity for violence increases through their teens and decreases after the early twenties. Low anxiety and high impulsivity are associated with a greater tendency for aggression. But what is the immediate trigger? It used to be held that aggressive acts are caused by frustration. While such a theory can explain acts of violence, it is not very helpful, since it will explain nearly everything. Most of us can be said to be frustrated by something, most of the time. In any case, aggression is not an automatic response to frustration: the individual takes into account whether the frustration is fair, whether violence would be relevant, and so on. But certain circumstances do make violence more likely - physiological arousal, aversive stimulation, fear, the presence of weapons. It is no coincidence that industrial countries where citizens have an almost automatic right to carry guns also have high homicide rates.

Aggression between groups raises rather different issues. The groups one belongs to affect how one sees oneself. Thus one thinks of oneself as a member of a particular nation, sex, profession, family, sports club, and so on. Because group membership contributes in this way to social identity, individuals tend to identify with groups that they perceive favourably, and to perceive favourably groups with which they identify. Members of one's own group are perceived more positively, and as more individually distinct, than members of outgroups. The difference between the ingroup and the outgroup tends to be magnified, and the group may elaborate its own rules and norms. Most groups of any size have an internal structure, with leaders and so forth.

Such factors affect the nature of aggression between groups. The leader may set the tone, or require this or that course of action. He or she may denigrate the outgroup as a means to stabilise his or her own position. The group members may vie amongst themselves for position or status, and this may affect their behaviour towards the outgroup. For instance, in a situation of incipient rioting, the individual who throws the first brick at the police, or who is most daring in action against the outgroup, gains kudos from other ingroup members. Aggressiveness is thus augmented by assertiveness. Violence can be contagious. The arousal, anonymity, and reduced responsibility in the group situation may exacerbate the tendency to show violent behaviour. And, perniciously, inter-group violence exploits not only aggressiveness but also the other side of human nature - the tendency to cooperate with other in-group members against the outgroup.

Now let us turn to international war, as exemplified by the two world wars. The distinction from intergroup conflicts is of course not absolute: such wars mark the end of a continuum in that they involve complex societies each with overlapping constituent sub-groups, in that the role of the leaders is paramount, and in that their complexity demands marked role differentiation.

Because of this role differentiation, war is best seen as an institution. Just as marriage is an institution with constituent roles of husband and wife, just as Parliament is an institution with constituent roles of Prime Minister, Members of Parliament, the voting public, and so on, so also can war be seen as an institution with numerous constituent roles - soldiers, generals, politicians, munition workers, medics, and so on. In an institution, the incumbents of each role have certain rights and certain duties: there are certain things that husbands and wives, Ministers and voters, are allowed to do and others they are expected to do. In the same way, incumbents of each of the roles in the institution of war have certain rights and duties. In major international wars the munition workers make bullets because it is their duty to do so. The transport workers convey the bullets from factory to combatants because it is their duty to do so. The combatants fight because it is their duty to fight and to kill. Aggressiveness plays little part in their motivation, nor does material gain. Fear may augment it in some instances. Cooperation with "brothers-in-arms" may be important. But duty is paramount. Aggressiveness does not cause killing in war; wars cause aggression.

Of course there are many intermediates between aggression between small groups and international war. The recent conflicts in the former Yugoslavia and Rwanda were only partially institutionalised, and naked aggression came to the surface. But in World War II and Vietnam simple aggression was usually not condoned - as at My Lai.

Wars are horrible, and bring with them suffering for the combatants involving the possibility or even probability of death, mutilation, blindness, and captivity. For civilian by-standers they bring suffering, chaos, often starvation, and irreplaceable loss for next-of-kin. For all there is lethal fall-out not only in the form of physical radiation but also in the frustration of defeat or the complacent self-righteousness of victory, in the cancer of revenge, the dehumanisation that too easily accompanies conflict, the devaluation of mercy. Somehow, we must eliminate wars, and to achieve that we must look not only at the immediate causes of wars, but also at what makes something that is so unspeakable acceptable as a means of settling disputes, at what supports war as an institution.

The factors involved are multiple. Some are everyday matters. The novels and films in which war is sanitised and blood and spilled guts concealed; which take the perspective of the winners, never the losers; which speak only of the heroics, never of the gut-crunching terror. The war toys which fascinate the young and teach them that war is a normal occupation for adults. The education which treats history as a succession of wars. Male chauvinism which glorifies war.

Other factors are more pervasive. Some nations have traditions of belliger-ence. Religions sometimes glorify aggression by using militaristic metaphors ("soldiers of Christ"), and glorify death in war by equating it with Christ's sacrifice on the Cross ("Greater love hath no man than this, that he lays down his life for his friends"). Nationalism uses propaganda which denigrates the members of other groups and plays on the readiness of individuals to fear strangers by portraying them as evil and sub-human.

And, perhaps most important of all, the military-industrial-scientific complex. Driven sometimes by honest patriotism, more often by ambition and greed, and sometimes by fat cats who will sell their products to the highest bidder without caring two pennies about the use to which they will be put, it can be seen as an institution in its own right with a nested series of sub-institutions, each with their constituent roles, each role having its associated rights and duties. The scientists strive to invent more deadly weapons and to convince the military of their value; the industrialists make them, sell them and, to cover their costs, do not confine themselves to their own military. Governments encourage widespread sales to help cover the overheads on their own purchases. Each institution is fuelled by the (in some ways understandable) assertiveness and ambition of the individuals involved.

Clearly, the issues are not simple. To reduce violence between individuals we have to ensure that their experiences are benign, and that means both educating parents and ensuring that the world is a fair world in which the parents can realise the unselfish sides of their own natures. A long-term job. To reduce warfare, we must influence not only individuals but also governments and through them the arms manufacturers. While avoiding the encroaching cultural uniformity imposed by rampant capitalism, we must inculcate tolerance (within limits) and understanding for others' values. More long-term issues. But the situation is by no means hopeless. Popular will can achieve a great deal, in some countries at least. Governments can be persuaded - or in due course they fall. Above all we must remember that humans are not inevitably aggressive, wars are not in our genes: empathy, selflessness, cooperation are less newsworthy but equally possible.

28

DECLARATION OF WAR
HANS MAGNUS ENZENSBERGER

In the backroom of a beer-cellar
where seven boozers have a meeting of minds,
there is war in the air; it is smoldering
in the day nursery; it is being bred
in the Academy of Science; it thrives
at the hands of the midwife
in Gori or in Braunau, in the Internet,
in the mosque; the tiny brain
of the patriotic bard will sweat it out;
because someone is deeply hurt,
because someone has a taste for it,
for goodness' sake war will rage,
for the colour of your skin,
in bunkers, for fun, by mistake,
because sacrifices have to be made
for our salvation, preferably by night,
because of the oilfields; since self-mutilation,
too, has its attractions, and since there is
money in it, war starts, in a delirium,
because of a football match lost;
far from it; for God's sake; really?;
although nobody really wanted it;
oh I see; just like that; for the heck of it;
heroically, and for lack of a better idea.

original translation by the author

WHEN ART MEETS POLITICS:
ORIGINAL EXPRESSION AND SOCIAL ISSUES
NADINE GORDIMER

WHEN ART MEETS POLITICS:
ORIGINAL EXPRESSION AND SOCIAL ISSUES
NADINE GORDIMER

THE arts are many, and their expression of social issues springs to mind from Picasso's *Guernica* via Goya as the apotheosis of wars, to – in film – Costa-Gavras and Semprun's *Z* as the apotheosis of junta oppression, Schlöndorff's *Tin Drum* as that of social deformation, the dwarfing of humanity during Nazism, to Kusturica's *Underground* and Neil Jordan's *The Crying Game* as that of conflict that continues above ground, even today, and Spike Lee's *Do The Right Thing* vision of racism in America.

As a writer, however, I shall naturally concentrate on our subject in relation to the art. I myself practise and know best in the work of my fellow writers, dead and alive – literature.

First a look back at writers in whom most obviously art meets politics, on different levels and in differing ways. One should begin with the Bible, of course, both Old Testament and New, the lyrical source-books of politics secular – the politics of tribal succession – and politics religious – the power struggles for the soul, between human beings and God. Then I pass over the centuries, the ancient Greeks and Dante, to *Uncle Tom's Cabin* and *Cry, The Beloved Country*. These two show how a sentimental story can be effective form of expression of a social issue, since, a century apart, Harriet Beecher Stowe's *Uncle Tom* and Alan Paton's *Reverend Kumalo* brought the issues of slavery and racism into the consciousness of millions of readers who might not have admitted these if presented any other way.

Black Ralph Ellison and James Baldwin despised sentiment as inadequate to express the realities of race prejudice, revealing the black persona as the one of whom *Nobody Knows My Name*, the *Invisible Man* rejected by whites.

Joseph Roth used the picaresque mode to epitomise patriotic hubris and the end of the Austro-Hungarian Empire with the von Trotta generations in *The Radetzky March*.

Malraux gave expression to the mood of *Days of Hope* in the doomed early resistance to fascism in the Spanish Civil War while Hemingway proposed the sexual stimulus of war as a social phenomenon – the earth moved by orgasm rather that by bombs.

Thomas Mann used the snowy isolation of a sanatorium in the Swiss alps to signify the complacency of a Europe skiing towards disaster, from which to pitch his antihere, Hans Castorp, into the 'universal feast of Death' which Mann saw as the 1914 war. Ariel Dorfman, with his play *Death and the Maiden* written in exile from Pinochet's Chile, reveals the social situation of a woman, in the reconciliation of an emerging democracy, confronted with her former torturer as house-guest.

I have lately, in a novel, *The House Gun*, explored the social significance of a *crime passionnel* in the world climate of urban violence we live in now. And Jorge Semprun is one who has interiorised the social and ideological conflicts of our time as autobiography in the valediction 'Adieu, vive clarté'.

Why have these writers and many others taken on themselves the meeting of art with socio-politics?

Günter Grass has an answer. He says: 'My professional life, my writing, all the things that interest me, have taught me that I cannot freely choose my subjects. For the most part my subjects were assigned to me by German history, by the war that was criminally started and conducted, and by the neverending consequences of that era. Thus my books are fatally linked to these subjects, and I am not the only one who has had this experience'.[1]

Indeed he is not. The rest of us are fatally linked to the political and social consequences of whatever our society, our country, that country's politics, may be, and further, to the flux and reflux of the globalisation we are beginning to live through. That is why original expression is inexorably linked to politics. It is, as Kafka wrote 'a leap out of murderers' row, it is a seeing of what is really taking place'.[2]

The next question is what is the effect of the writer's and artist's original expression of social issues on the individual consciousness of society?

The way in which art's expression of social and political issues is of use to mankind lies surely in the engagement of the artist with these issues at his or her deepest level of independent, searching understanding, the ability of the creative imagination to mine for the unexpressed in human motivation the unadmitted, the necessary insights that the facts can never reveal.

This is not to deny that writers and artists themselves have been and are hotly divided on whether or not art should be involved with an imperative of political and social issues. Proust judged that such issues 'whether the Dreyfus affair or the war' simply 'furnished excuses to the writers for not deciphering... that book within them'[3]. The Marxist critic Ernst Fischer, cuttingly pronounced 'The feature common to all significant artists and writers in the capitalist world is their inability to come to terms with the social reality that surrounds them.[4]' Picasso – never at a loss for words: 'What do you think an artist is? An imbecile who has nothing but eyes if he is a painter, or ears if he is a musician, or a lyre at every level of his heart if he is a poet... Quite the contrary, he is at the same time a political being, constantly aware of what goes on in the world... and he cannot help being shaped by it... painting is not interior decoration. It is an instrument of war for attack and defense against the enemy'.[5]

Flaubert complains: 'I have always tried to live in an ivory tower, but a tide of shit is beating at its walls, threatening to undermine it... it's not a question of politics but of a mental state of France'.[6]

George Steiner, speaking of writing under totalitarian rule, calls for the writer to stop writing 'a few miles down the road from the death camp... nothing speaks louder that the unwritten poem'[7]. But hear Neruda: 'I felt a pressing need to write a central poem that would bring together the historical events, the geographical situations, the life... of our peoples'[8]. And Rilke, looking at Cézanne painting, exclaims: 'Suddenly one has the right eyes'[9], and Milan Kundera sees writers and artists as vital witnesses, saying of the 20th century as an age marked by tyranny '…people regard those days as an era of political trials, persecution, forbidden books and legalised murder. But we who remember must bear witness; it was not only an epoch of terror, but also an epoch of lyricism, ruled hand in hand by the hangman and the poet'.[10]

Finally, for us – writers and artists bringing original expression to politics and social issues at the end of this century where neither socialism nor capitalism has achieved justice and human fulfilment for all – Czeslaw Milosz has the rubric:

'Ill at ease in the tyranny, ill at ease in the republic
In the one I longed for freedom, in the other for the end of corruption'.[11]

Notes

1   Günter Grass. In conversation with Nadine Gordimer, 1997

2   Franz Kafka. *Kafka's Diaries* 1922

3   Marcel Proust. *A La Recherche du Temps Perdu*

4   Ernst Fischer. *The Necessity of Art*

5   Pablo Picasso. *Lettres Françaises*

6   Gustave Flaubert. Letter to Turgeneve, 13 November 1872,
     The Letters of Gustave Flaubert 1857-1880. Ed. Francis Steegmuller

7   George Steiner. *Language and Silence*

8   Pablo Neruda. My notebooks do not give the source, probably his autobiography.

9   Rainer Maria Rilke. *Letters on Cézanne*. Translated by Joel Agee.

10   Milan Kundera. *Life is Elsewhere*

11   Czeslaw Milosz. *'To Raja Raó' Selected Poems 1980*

34

VISIT
HANS MAGNUS ENZENSBERGER

What do you want?
I'm the good Samaritan,
coming from the cleaner's.
I did not call you.
Where's your I.D.?
I'm your salvation.
No need for papers.
Why are you trembling?
What are you afraid of?
I hear noises.
That's just a coat-hanger
rambling down.
And what is this smell?
Exhaust fumes. Balm.
Balm for your wounds.
I want my lawyer.
He will not help you.
That was no coat-hanger!
These are not fumes!
I am the pest control,
the first aid team,
the extreme unction.
I want a fair deal.
That's not my business.
I want revenge.
I take it.
My lips are sealed.
That is all right by me.
I bring what you are looking for,
peace and quiet.

original translation by the author

36

THE LAST JUDGEMENT

STARING INTO THE ABYSS
JOHN SPURLING

"What if this present were the world's last night?" asks John Donne in one of his Holy Sonnets. Our time is almost up by his arithmetic. Preaching in St Paul's Cathedral on Christmas Day, 1625, he noted that it was "ordinarily received" that there would be 6000 years between

> "the Creation of Adam, and the last note of the blowing of the
> Trumpets to judgement… 2000 yeares of nature between the Creation
> and the giving of the Law by Moses, and 2000 yeares of the Law
> between that and the comming of Christ, and 2000 yeares of Grace
> and Gospell between Christ first and his second comming…".

But for most of us the terrors of a Last Judgement have been largely outstripped by reality. Except that hell is supposed to go on for ever, what worse could a divine Judge hand down to humanity than humanity has handed down to itself in the 20th century? At the end of the last century Friedrich Nietzsche wrote, in *Thus Spake Zarathustra*:

> "Man is the cruellest of all the animals. His happiest moments have
> been spent at tragedies, bull-fights and crucifixions; and his invention
> of hell was entirely based on his idea of heaven on earth."

Indeed it is precisely our idealism - our need for gods, ethical systems, patriotisms and social ideologies - that makes us so much crueller than other animals. By first envisaging a better world and then trying to enforce it, either here or hereafter, we extend Nature's casual bloodshed into morally justified mayhem. Animals would surely laugh - or cry - if they understood the way we use the word 'human' to mean something kinder, gentler, morally better than 'animal'.

The punishments associated with the idea of a Last Judgement are necessarily based, like all human images, on what we already do or would like to do. There is some risk even in contemplating the Last Judgement, since its screen of moral rectitude conceals a riot of instincts and impulses which we may find ourselves too closely caught up in: violence, resentment, anger, revenge. No one has ever created a steadier vision of Hell than Dante, but he could not resist the opportunity to pay off scores against his own personal and political enemies. "The hero who fights with monsters", said Nietszche in *Beyond Good and Evil* "must take care not to become a monster himself. If you stare too long into the abyss, the abyss will stare into you."

This is no longer a problem confined to heroes. Everyone now can watch highlights from whatever abyss is in the news. Add the steady stream of stories about all the perils attending our imperfect knowledge and control of forces we have begun to interfere with, and it starts to look as if we are actually living in a kind of soap opera called The Last Judgement.

But although the scale of our predicament has increased so alarmingly, it is essentially the same as it always has been: we are alive, we don't know why, and we are certain to die one way or another. Philosophies ask questions about this and sometimes try to answer them; religions claim to answer them; but artists and writers transform the questions into images and stories which marvellously conjure vitality, meaning and even aesthetic pleasure out of gloom, nihilism and anxiety. And because there is no such thing as 'progress' in art or literature, we can go on accumulating images and stories instead of discarding and replacing them, as we have to do with most other things. Jorge Luis Borges remarked that writers only add a few words or pages to the great book of the world. Anthony Caro has now added to the great visual tradition of the Last Judgement, which, since it has been as much a literary as a visual subject, I have flagged with some passages from the great book of the world. The translations cannot do justice to the originals, but they are as exact as possible and my own.

THE BELL TOWER

40 No man is an Iland, intire of it selfe; every man is a peece of the Continent, a part of the maine … any mans death diminishes me, because I am involved in Mankinde; And therefore never send to know for whom the bell tolls; It tolls for thee.

John Donne, *Devotions Upon Emergent Occasions, XVII*

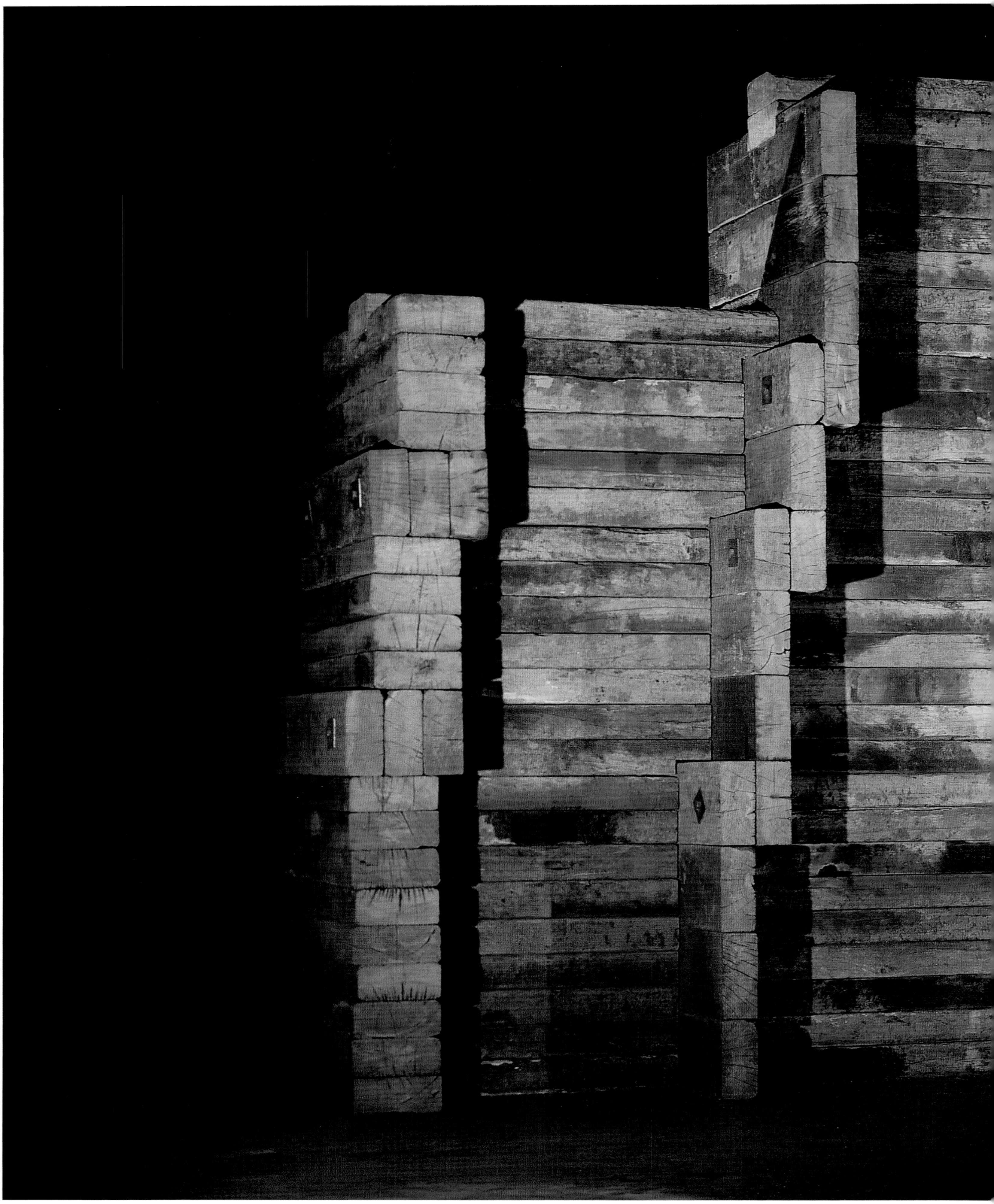

THE DOOR OF DEATH

44   Night and day black Pluto's door stands open.

Virgil, *The Aeneid*, Book VI

CHARON

46 There, coming in a boat towards us
was an old man thatched with white hair,
screaming: "Bad cess to you, miserable souls!
No hope for you of ever seeing sky again!
I'm here to ferry you to the far bank,
to everlasting dark, fire and ice..."
Those tired and naked souls changed colour
and their teeth were chattering
as they took in his brutal words.
They cursed God and their parents,
the human race, the place, the time, the seed
of their conception and their birth...
The demon Charon, with red-hot eyes,
beckoned them on, gathered them all in:
and clouted the ditherers with his oar.

Dante, *Inferno*, Canto III

48 Here, in the deep abyss, the muddy flood
seethes and swirls and belches its sludge into Cocytus.
The horrible guardian of these waters is Charon,
squalid, repulsive...
He propels his rust-coloured hulk with sails and a pole,
And ferries the dead...

Virgil, *Aeneid,* Book VI

HELL IS A CITY

50   Hell is a city much like London -
A populous and smoky city.

P B Shelley, *Peter Bell the Third*, part 3

God the first garden made, and the first city Cain.

Abraham Cowley, *The Garden*

HELL IS A CITY

52 All four lanes were heavy with traffic... he could see the island of Manhattan off to the left. The towers were jammed together so tightly, he could feel the mass and stupendous weight. Just think of the millions, from all over the globe, who yearned to be on that island, in those towers, in those narrow streets! There it was, the Rome, the Paris, the London of the twentieth century, the city of ambition, the dense magnetic rock, the irresistible destination of all those who insist on being *where things are happening...*

Tom Wolfe, *The Bonfire of the Vanities*

The City is of Night, but not of Sleep;

James Thomson, *The City of Dreadful Night*

WITHOUT MERCY

54 The Duke of Monmouth's rebellion against King James II in 1685 was crushed at the battle of Sedgmoor in Somerset.

Somersetshire, the chief seat of the rebellion, had been reserved for the last and most fearful vengeance. In this country two hundred and thirty-three prisoners were in a few days hanged, drawn, and quartered. At every spot where two roads met, on every market-place, on the green of every large village which had furnished Monmouth with soldiers, ironed corpses clattering in the wind, or heads and quarters stuck on poles, poisoned the air, and made the traveller sick with horror.

Lord Macaulay, *The History of England*

56

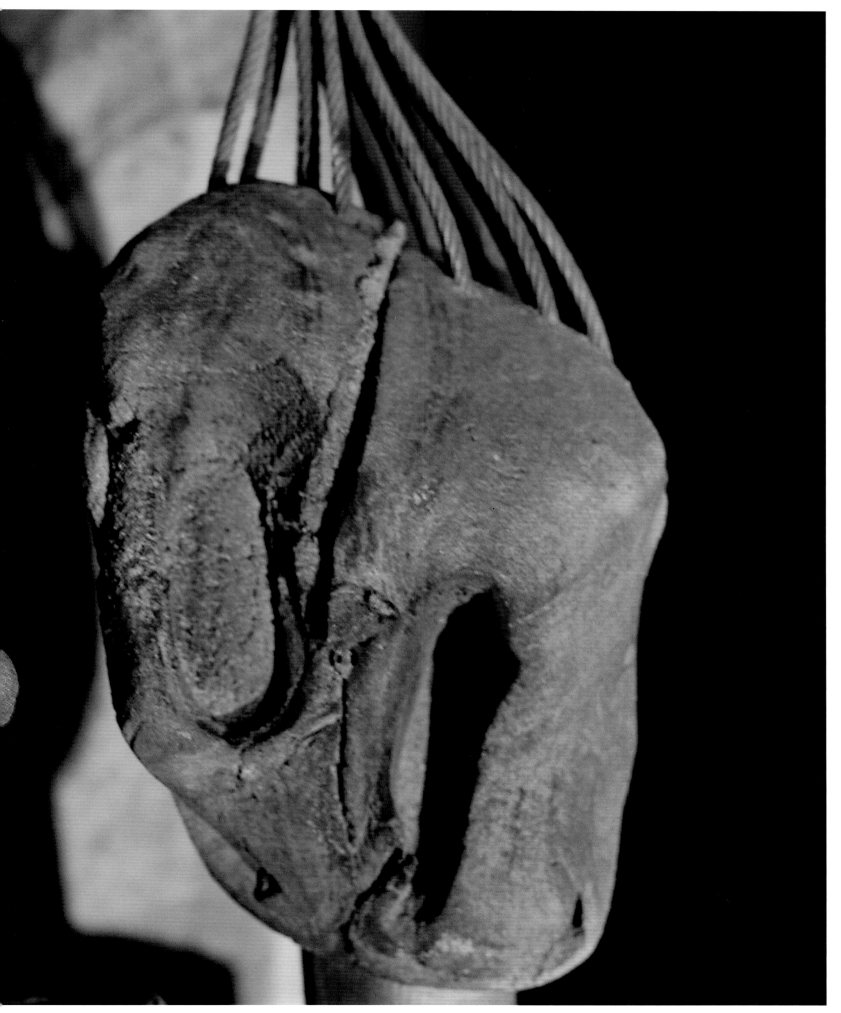

UNKNOWN SOLDIER

Wilfred Owen was killed while commanding a company of infantry on the bank of the Sambre Canal seven days before the Armistice that ended the First World War. His poem *Strange Meeting* ends:

I am the enemy you killed, my friend.
I knew you in this dark; for so you frowned
Yesterday through me as you jabbed and killed.
I parried; but my hands were loath and cold.
Let us sleep now . . .

60 Keith Douglas was killed while commanding a tank troop during the
Normandy landings in 1944, towards the end of the Second World War:

Now in my dial of glass appears
the soldier who is going to die.
He smiles, and moves about in ways
his mother knows, habits of his.
The wires touch his face: I cry
NOW. Death, like a familiar, hears
and look, has made a man of dust
of a man of flesh...

from *How to Kill*

SHADES OF NIGHT

62 Faust:

Ah, Faustus.
Now hast thou but one bare hour to live,
And then thou must be damn'd perpetually!
Stand still, you ever-moving spheres of heaven,
That time may cease, and midnight never come...
*O lente, lente currite, noctis equi!** *
The stars move still, time runs, the clock will strike,
The devil will come, and Faustus must be damn'd.

Christopher Marlowe, *Doctor Faustus*

** Go slowly, slowly, horses of night!*

66 And we are here as on a darkling plain
Swept with confused alarms of struggle and flight,
Where ignorant armies clash by night.

Matthew Arnold, *Dover Beach*

ELYSIAN FIELDS

Homer puts Elysium on the far edge of the earth. In Virgil's *Aeneid*,
six or seven centuries later, it is part of the underworld.

Now they came to the region of happiness, the lovely green
Lawns and blissful arbours of the Elysian Woods.
Here the air is fresher and the land bathed
In brilliant light - having its own sun and stars...
Here live those who died fighting for their country,
Priests who committed no sins, poets and prophets
Whose words did honour to their calling,
Artists and inventors who made life more civilised,
All those that deserve to be remembered.

The Aeneid, Book VI

TEIRESIAS

70   Teiresias was a mythical Greek seer, blind, but endowed with inward sight. In Sophocles' play *King Oedipus* Teiresias tells Oedipus the truth he doesn't want to hear, that he murdered his predecessor as King of Thebes. Even after his death Teiresias was supposed to retain his powers. Homer's redoubtable wanderer, Odysseus, trying to get home from Troy, is told:

"You must go to the halls of Hades and fearsome Persephone,
to consult the soul of the blind prophet, Theban Teiresias."
His understanding is as good as ever it was,
for, though he is dead, Persephone has given intelligence
and reason to him alone. The rest are flitting shadows.

Homer, *The Odyssey*, Book X

72 For the Christian Dante, 2000 years later, Teiresias has become one of the sorcerers in the Eighth Circle of Hell and is less famous for his wisdom than for having once changed sex. Virgil, Dante's guide, points him out:

Look! There's Teiresias who switched his semblance
When, born a man, he changed into a woman
And every part of her took on a new appearance.

Dante, *Inferno*

TORTURE BOX

74 The torturer enjoying himself, the martyr moaning;
The festival spiced and scented with blood;
The despot inflamed with the poison of power,
And the people in love with the brutalising whip;
. . .
This is the never-ending news of the world.

Charles Baudelaire, *Le Voyage*

76   The pattern is for agents to pick someone up from work, or at night
from his house. No explanations are proffered as there would be in an
official killing. What one assumes to be the corpse is brought back
weeks or maybe months later and delivered to the head of the family in
a sealed box. A death certificate is produced for signature to the effect
that the person has died of fire, swimming, or other such accident.
Someone is allowed to accompany police and box for a ceremony, but at
no time is he or she permitted to see the corpse. The cost of the
proceedings is demanded in advance, and the whole thing is over within
hours of the first knock on the door...

Samir al-Khalil, *Republic of Fear: Saddam's Iraq*

STILL LIFE - SKULLS

78 On his last mornings Cézanne clarified this idea of death into a heap of bony brainpans to which the eyeholes added a bluish notion. I can still hear him reciting to me, one evening along the Arc River, the quatrain by Verlaine:

For in this sluggish world
Constantly prey to remorse
The only rational laughter
Is that of death's-heads

Joachim Gasquet, *Cézanne*, 1921, quoted by Françoise Cachin in the catalogue to an exhibition of Cézanne's work.

80 August 19, 1979. Pol Pot, the leader of the Khmer Rouge regime overthrown by the invading Vietnamese seven months ago, has today been sentenced to death for the genocide of the Cambodian people during his four years in power.

Millions of skulls in mounds dotting the Cambodian countryside testify to the ferocity of Pol Pot's campaign to wipe out Cambodia's middle class and intellectuals . . .

Chronicle of the 20th Century, edited by Derrik Mercer

FLESH

82   They ask me, in the streets,
Why I go gaping at the whores,
Smoking my cigar in the sun,
What I am doing with my youth,
And after three years of idleness
What I have to show for my sleepless nights...

Alfred de Musset, *A Julie*

GREED AND ENVY

84 The people at the slot machines inside seemed to work by similar mechanisms. They fed in thin quarters and dollars with their left hands and pulled levers with their right like assembly-line workers in a money factory. There were smudge eyed boys so young that they hadn't begun to shave yet, and women with workmen's gloves on their lever hands, some of them so old and weary that they leaned on the machines to stay upright. The money factory was a hard place to work.

Ross Macdonald, *Black Money*

'Tis a common disease, and almost natural to us, as Tacitus holds, to envy another man's prosperity. And 'tis in most men an incurable disease... "Every other sin hath some pleasure annexed to it, or will admit of an excuse; envy alone wants both. Other sins last but for a while; the gut may be satisfied, anger remits, hatred hath an end, envy never ceaseth." (Cardan, Bk. 1 On wisdom).

Robert Burton, *The Anatomy of Melancholy*

86 . . . who *was* Mr Bounderby? . . . He was a rich man: banker, merchant, manufacturer, and what not. A big, loud man, with a stare, and a metallic laugh . . . A man with a great puffed head and forehead, swelled veins in his temples . . . A man who could never sufficiently vaunt himself a self-made man . . . So, Mr Bounderby threw on his hat . . . and with his hands in his pockets, sauntered out into the hall. "I never wear gloves", it was his custom to say, "I didn't climb up the ladder in *them*. Shouldn't be so high up, if I had".

Charles Dickens, *Hard Times*

SACRIFICE

88 And when I made my prayers and petitions
To the hosts of the dead, I took and slaughtered
The sheep, and their dark blood ran into the pit.
Then the souls of the dead crowded up from Erebus…

Homer, *The Odyssey*, Book XI

SALOMÉ DANCES

92 But when Herod's birthday was kept, the daughter of Herodias danced
before them and pleased Herod. Whereupon he promised with an oath to
give her whatsoever she would ask. And she, being instructed of her
mother, said, Give me here John Baptist's head in a charger. And the king
was sorry: nevertheless for the oath's sake, and them which sat with him at
meat, he commanded it to be given her.

And he sent, and beheaded John in the prison. And his head was brought in
a charger, and given to the damsel: and she brought it to her mother.

St Matthew's Gospel, 14

94 Salomé:

Ah, thou wouldst not suffer me to kiss thy mouth, Jokanaan.
Well! I will kiss it now. I will bite it with my teeth as one bites a ripe fruit.
Yes, I will kiss thy mouth, Jokanaan... Thou wouldst have none of me,
Jokanaan. Thou didst reject me. Thou didst speak evil words against me.
Thou didst treat me as a harlot, as a wanton, me, Salomé, daughter of
Herodias, Princess of Judaea! Well, Jokanaan, I still live, but thou, thou art
dead, and thy head belongs to me... Ah, Jokanaan, thou wert the only man
that I have loved.

Oscar Wilde, *Salomé*

95

PRISONERS

96   They chain'd us each to a column stone,
And we were three - yet each alone;
We could not move a single pace,
We could not see each other's face,
But with that pale and livid light
That made us strangers in our sight...

Lord Byron, *The Prisoner of Chillon*

98   I never saw a man who looked
With such a wistful eye
Upon that little tent of blue
Which prisoners call the sky,
And at every drifting cloud that went
With sails of silver by.

Oscar Wilde, *The Ballad of Reading Gaol*

CONFESSION

Moslem law is never completely satisfied till the criminal confess.

Sir Richard Burton, footnote in *One Thousand and One Nights*, Vol. 1

… the Christians formed a numerous and disciplined society; and the jurisdiction of their laws and magistrates was strictly exercised over the minds of the faithful. The loose wanderings of the imagination were gradually combined by creeds and confessions… and the episcopal successors of the apostles inflicted the censures of the church on those who deviated from the orthodox belief.

Edward Gibbon, *Decline and Fall of the Roman Empire*, Chapter XXI

CIVIL WAR

102 Wallenstein:

What? Shall this town become a field of slaughter,
And brother-killing Discord, fire-eyed,
Be let loose through its streets to roam and rage?
Shall the decision be delivered over
To deaf remorseless Rage, that hears no leader?
Here is not room for battle, only for butchery.

The Death of Wallenstein, Coleridge's English version
of Schiller's play about the Thirty Years War

I saw a sniper carrying a Simonov rifle leave his position in a
ruined block of flats... When he looked at me his eyes were as
dead as the small child he had almost certainly killed that day in
a sniping attack on a Sarajevo street.

General Sir Michael Rose, *Fighting for Peace*

'Brother-killing discord' is central to all Shakespeare's tragedies
and history-plays. In *Julius Caesar* it is unleashed by Caesar's assassination.
Mark Antony prophesies over the corpse of his friend and patron:

Domestic fury and fierce civil strife
Shall cumber all the parts of Italy;
Blood and destruction shall be so in use,
And dreadful objects so familiar,
That mothers shall but smile when they behold
Their infants quartered with the hands of war,
All pity chok'd with custom of fell deeds;
And Caesar's spirit, ranging for revenge,
With Ate by his side come hot from hell,
Shall in these confines with a monarch's voice
Cry havoc and let slip the dogs of war...

JUDAS

108   He sees nothing but blackness, like a marble tomb.
The Earth without lights, without stars, without sign of dawn
Without light for the soul, as it still is,
Shuddered. - In the wood he heard footsteps,
And saw lurking there the torch of Judas.

Alfred de Vigny, *Le Mont des Oliviers*

I have been damaged since then,
As the corruption of the times took hold,
And, stabbing at the heart of citizens
And optimists, grief grew into shame.
So everything I trusted,
I have long since betrayed.
Since then I have lost touch
With man, just as they all have.

Boris Pasternak, *Change*

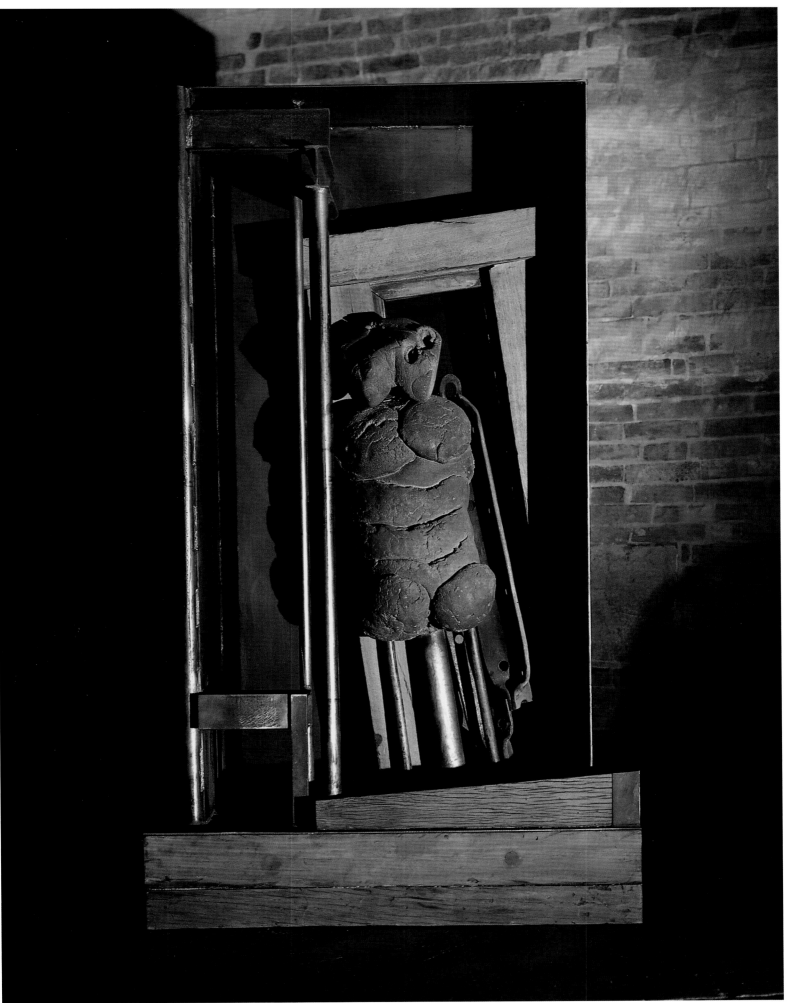

TRIBUNAL

110 Many prominent men, all the military and many civilian leaders, were tried *in camera*; many were executed without trial because they could not be brought to admit and recant crimes of which they had not been guilty. But all those unfortunates on whom the limelight was turned appeared in sackcloth and ashes, loudly confessing their sins, calling themselves sons of Belial and praising *de profundis* the Superman whose feet were crushing them into dust. A horrified and stultified nation was made to echo in one voice the refrain: 'Shoot the mad dogs!' with which the prosecutor Vyshinsky invariably wound up his denunciations. The confessions of the defendants were the only basis for the proceedings and the verdicts. Not a single piece of evidence that could be verified by means of normal legal procedure was presented.

Isaac Deutscher, describing the Russian trials of the 1930s
in *Stalin: a Political Biography*

112 Such ghastly visions had I of despair
And tyranny, and implements of death,
And long orations which in dreams I pleaded
Before unjust Tribunals, with a voice
Labouring, a brain confounded, and a sense
Of treachery and desertion in the place
The holiest that I knew of, my own soul.

Wordsworth's *The Prelude*

POISON CHAMBER

114 In Homer's *Iliad*, the Greek god Hephaistos is commissioned to make new armour for her son Achilles. The huge bronze shield is covered with wonderful scenes in relief. No longer so in the 1950s, however, according to W H Auden:

> She looked over his shoulder
> For vines and olive trees,
> Marble well-governed cities
> And ships upon untamed seas,
> But there on the shining metal
> His hands had put instead
> An artificial wilderness
> And a sky like lead.

The Shield of Achilles

116 Slowly the poison the whole blood stream fills.
It is not the effort nor the failure tires.
The waste remains, the waste remains and kills.

William Empson, *Missing Dates*

THE FURIES

118 The Furies in Greek mythology - also called the Eumenides (Kindly Ones) - were the old avenging gods of the earth. In the last play of Aeschylus' Oresteian trilogy, the Priestess of Apollo at Delphi finds the Furies inside the shrine at Delphi:

… seated in chairs,
Asleep, a monstrous crew of women.
Not women… Gorgons… Harpies…
But without wings, black, utterly loathsome -
Their breath thick, a disgusting snoring -
Filth dropping from their eyes…

Aeschylus, *Eumenides*

120 Dante, guided by the Roman poet Virgil, meets them in Hell. "They are the image", writes Dorothy Sayers, "of the fruitless remorse which does not lead to penitence":

There suddenly I saw a triple form,
three hellish Furies, the colour of blood,
with the shape and characteristics of women,
... their shrieks were so ear-splitting
that I clung to the poet in fear.

Inferno, Canto IX

JACOB'S LADDER

122   And Jacob went out from Beersheba, and went toward Haran. And he lighted upon a certain place, and tarried there all night, because the sun was set; and he took of the stones of that place, and put them for his pillows, and lay down in that place to sleep.

And he dreamed, and behold a ladder set up on the earth, and the top of it reached to heaven: and behold the angels of God ascending and descending on it. And behold, the Lord stood above it, and said, I am the Lord God of Abraham thy father, and the God of Isaac: the land whereon thou liest, to thee will I give it, and to thy seed...

And Jacob awaked out of his sleep, and he said, Surely the Lord is in this place; and I knew it not. And he was afraid, and said, How dreadful is this place! This is none other but the house of God, and this is the gate of heaven.

Genesis, 28

THE LAST TRUMP

124   ... the trumpet shall sound, and the dead shall be raised incorruptible, and we shall be changed.

First Epistle of Paul to the Corinthians, 15, 52

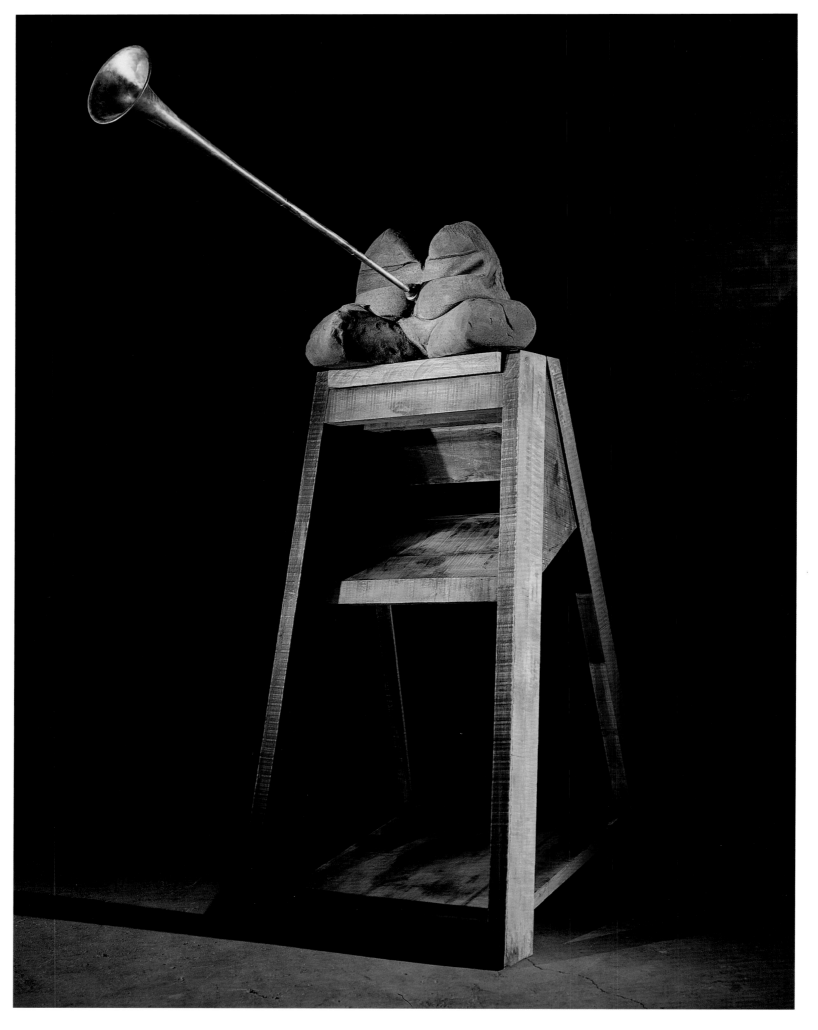

128 At the round earth's imagin'd corners, blow
Your trumpets, Angels, and arise, arise
From death, you numberlesse infinities
Of soules, and to your scattred bodies goe...

John Donne, *Holy Sonnets, VII*

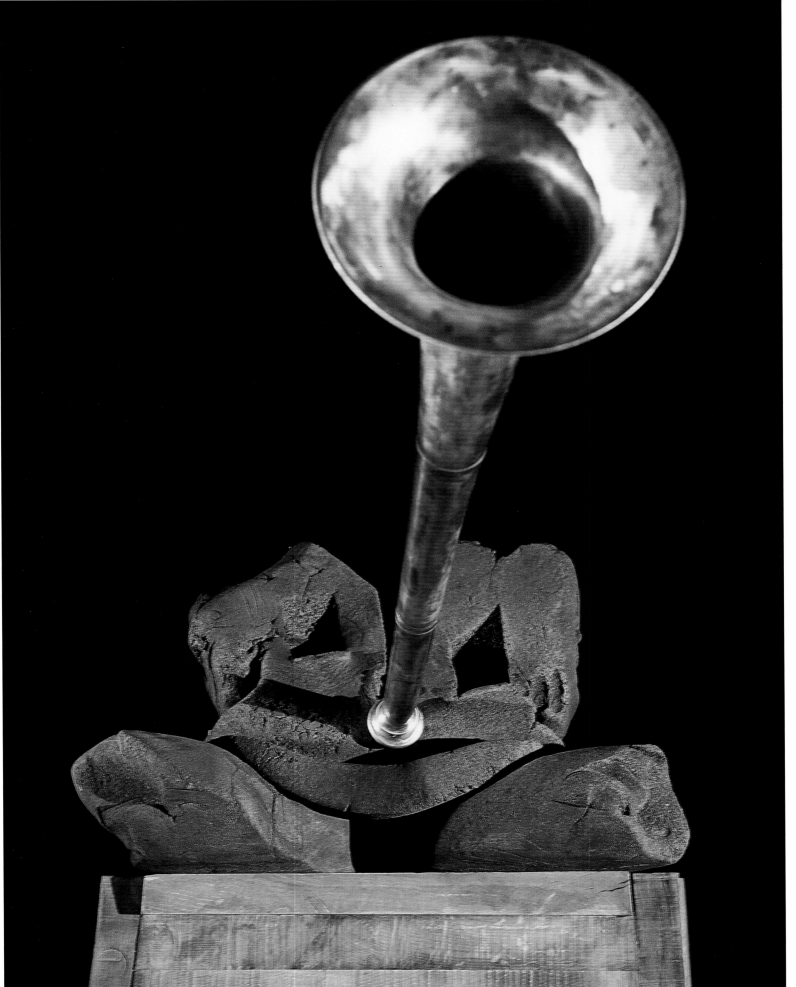

GATE OF HEAVEN

130 Blessed are they that do his commandments, that they may have right to the tree of life, and may enter in through the gates into the city.

The Revelation of St John the Divine, 22

Now I saw in my dream that these two men went in at the gate: and lo, as they entered, they were transfigured, and they had raiment put on that shone like gold. There were also that met them with harps and crowns, and gave them to them, - the harps to praise withal, and the crowns in token of honour. Then I heard in my dream that all the bells in the city rang again for joy....

John Bunyan, *The Pilgrim's Progress, Part 1*

ART AND MORALITY
PETER BAELZ

132

IN her memorable *Leslie Stephen Lecture for 1967*[1] the Oxford novelist and philosopher, Iris Murdoch, who died earlier this year, painted a powerful picture of the moral life, not as a matter of contractual and utilitarian convenience, but as a process of purification of the human consciousness in response to the transcendent claims of truth, beauty and goodness.

She began with two unargued but not altogether implausible assumptions. First, that the human psyche is inherently selfish, and that in its instinctive drive for self-protection against the harsh demands of reality it creates for itself a fantasy-world of illusion, indulgence and consolation. Second, that the world is complete in itself and patently purposeless, a combination of necessity and chance; and that 'if there is any kind of sense or unity in human life; and the dream of this does not cease to haunt us; it . . . must be sought within a human experience which has nothing outside it.'

Despite its significant contribution to political liberalism, Iris Murdoch rejects the post-Kantian model of the independent and morally autonomous individual who, under the banner of freedom and sincerity, turns his back on tradition and in an act of promethean wilfulness creates his own values, incidentally deriving thereby a thrill of surreptitious pride as a value-bearing alien in a valueless and indifferent world.

Over against this view of an ultimately arbitrary morality, Iris Murdoch argues that fundamental human values are discovered, not invented. Some manifestations of human consciousness and activity really are more praise-worthy than others. Virtue does not hang loose above or around our heads: it is 'tied on to the human condition'.

In the moral life the struggle against self-indulgent and self-consoling fantasy and the commitment to objectivity and truth call forth the virtues of humility, discernment, justice and compassion. The claims of a human excellence that resists the clamour for self-satisfaction and the instinctive desire to manipulate and control what is other than oneself are a revelation of true goodness. Goodness in its purity is a norm that transcends its varied and imperfect manifestations in human life: nevertheless, it exercises an abiding presence and authority as a magnetic and unifying source, criterion and goal.

The whole lecture merits careful study. Its reinterpretation of the Platonic myth of the cave, where shadows of artifacts are happily taken for real objects, and of the soul's reorientation and ascent to the light of day, provides a powerful and persuasive metaphor of the moral life. Its focus on the need for a conversion of the imagination and a commitment to objectivity highlights basic features of the moral pilgrimage. Its association of the ultimate indefinability of the Good 'with the unsystematic and inexhaustible variety of the world and the pointlessness of virtue' is a valiant attempt to preserve the absoluteness of goodness without emptying the concept of all significance. While unashamedly commending a transcendent ideal for human endeavour, it never forgets the empirical limitations and shortcomings of human nature.

Our immediate concern, however, with this lecture is not – or, at any rate, not directly – with its description of the moral life and its defence of a specific ideal of human excellence. Rather, it is with its comparison of morality with art and its insistence that in the arts we can see the essential human virtues displayed, as it were, in all their transparency. For Iris Murdoch art itself is, or should be, a moral activity.

She begins – because here, she suggests, the point of her argument is more readily accessible – by indicating what she conceives to be the analogy, and indeed the overlap, between the challenge of morality and the experience of natural beauty. The following often quoted passage deserves to be quoted once again:

> I am looking out of my window in an anxious and resentful state of mind, oblivious of my surroundings, brooding perhaps on some damage done to my prestige. Then suddenly I observe a hovering kestrel. In a moment everything is altered. The brooding self with its hurt vanity has disappeared. There is nothing now but kestrel. And when I return to thinking of the other matter it seems less important.

In the recognition of the sheer otherness and beauty of the kestrel a new attitude is engendered and a new source of moral energy released. This takes place, not through some arbitrary fiat of the will, but through the transformation of the human consciousness, whereby preoccupation with the fantasies and fixations of the self give way to a self-forgetful concentration on the being and beauty of the kestrel. Taking 'a self-forgetful pleasure in the sheer alien pointless independent existence of animals, birds, stones and trees' can itself be a step on a more comprehensive moral pilgrimage.

The moral pattern that can be discerned in the experience of nature can also be discerned in the experience of art. Good art – that is, art which 'affords us a pure delight in the independent existence of what is excellent' and presents us with a 'perfection of form which invites unpossessive contemplation and resists absorption into the selfish dream life of the consciousness', is not only 'a sacrament or a source of good energy', but, as a human rather than a natural product, shows us the virtues of humanity in the production as well as in the appreciation of beauty. Good artists have their skills. They have learned and mastered the potentialities of the medium in which they work. But they also have their virtues. 'The good artist, in relation to his art, is brave, truthful, patient, humble'. Only as such can he recognise and communicate 'what we are usually too selfish and too timid to recognise, the minute and absolutely random detail of the world', and communicate it 'together with a sense of unity and form'.

The virtues that are requisite for the making of good art are also requisite for the appreciation of good art. 'Art transcends selfish and obsessive limitations of personality and can enlarge the sensibility of its consumer. It is a kind of goodness by proxy. Most of all it exhibits to us the connection, in *human* beings, of clear realistic vision with compassion. The realism of a great artist is not a photographic realism, it is essentially both pity and justice'.

Such a view of the relationship between morality and art as Iris Murdoch proposes, according to which both morality and art are, in their different but analogous ways, responses to a transcendent and authoritive reality, is widely regarded today as pretentious and illiberal. God was long ago pronounced to be dead. Now humanity too has been deconstructed. Nothing is left with any claim to authority in face of the random predilections of the isolated individual except, perhaps, sincerity – the right (or even the duty?) to speak and act just as one happens to feel and think.

It is not difficult to understand why such a rejection of a transcendent moral universe should have occurred. Apart from the variety of conflicting moral judgements and the consequent suspicion that values are no more than private preferences, talk of transcendent and authoritative values can all too easily mask pretensions of power, ideology and manipulation. This being so, the unmasking of power and the defence of individual rights become a moral necessity. However, all too easily this affirmation of individual rights can take upon itself the character of a power struggle. In this process it defines itself in the very terms of what, fundamentally, it seeks to reject. Freedom is now identified with self-assertion, creativity with self-expression, communication with ideological propaganda. In short, the inter-subjective universe of personal responsiveness and responsibility, of listening, conversation and mutual regard, gives way to a chaos of confrontation, rhetoric and alienation. In place of a community of friends we are confronted with a crowd of strangers, in place of a culture of trust with a climate of suspicion. In this way the abuses of power which hid themselves under the banner of authority are succeeded by abuses of power hiding under the banner of freedom. The disciplines and courtesies of an open, responsive and responsible community are replaced by the strident clamours of a self-enclosed and outwardly hostile subjectivity.

In aspiring to a deeper and more authentic humanity sincerity is not enough. It must be extended and transformed into integrity, a more demanding and more comprehensive virtue which embraces the objective as well as the subjective and acknowledges, beyond the needs and aspirations of the self, the reality and claims of what is other than the self. Integrity includes but goes beyond sincerity. It springs from what the moral philosopher Helen Oppenheimer once called a 'kind of patient and skilful focusing of fact and value together'[2]. It combines the engaged subjectivity of compassion with the detached objectivity of thought and calls for both sensitivity of feeling and dispassion of judgement. Integrity entails a continuing search for a kind of 'wholeness' of appreciation in terms of what is judged to give to human life its ultimate and sustaining significance.

Can something analogous be claimed for artistic integrity? Or is the most that we may look for in the work of an artist a mastery of artistic medium combined with a sincerity of self-expression?

The artist does not work in a vacuum. The restraints with which he is presented are, in the first place, the material constraints of the medium in which he works – constraints which he can, to a greater or less degree, master by developing his practical skills. There are, however, other and non-material constraints presented by the character of his work as a work of art – constraints such as its otherness and self-existence, or its power to stand over against and even to resist his own preconceptions and preferences; its intrinsic harmony of form and content ('have I got it quite "right"?'); its heightened evocation of the contingent and particular combined with its intimation of the necessary and universal. These are constraints which cannot be 'mastered'. They are not overcome by the acquisition of the relevant skill. They remain constant, inherent in the work of art itself and to be discerned, acknowledged and heeded rather than eliminated. They mark out the parameters of the world of art. Like the language of morality, the language of art possesses its own distinctive syntax and logic, different from that of the market-place or the everyday struggle for survival and success. As the philosopher Ludwig Wittgenstein put it:

> The work of art is the object seen *sub specie aeternitatis*; and the good
> life is the world seen *sub specie aeternitatis*.
> This is the connection between art and ethics.
> The usual way of looking at things sees objects as it were from the
> midst of them, the view *sub specie aeternitatis* from the outside.
> In such a way they have the whole world as background.[3]

Restraints such as these, it should be noted, do not detract from the artist's freedom and creativity. Imagination, for instance, is more fundamental and more 'creative' than 'originality'. 'I do not believe' wrote Mary Warnock, philosopher and educator,

> that children exercise imagination more by having a set of hand-bells
> put before them, or a glockenspiel, and being told to make their own
> music than by listening to music with a receptive ear. I do not believe
> that there is anything uniquely valuable (though it may have value)
> in getting children to write or draw things which are to be *original*...
> The fact is that if imagination is creative in all its uses, then children
> will be creating their own meanings and interpretations of things as
> much by looking at them as by making them.[4]

In other words, imagination is receptive before it is active and has to learn the language of art before it can say anything of artistic value. True creativity is both traditional and radical. As a critic once wrote of Michael Tippett's Fourth Symphony, 'He works within the tradition but shatters the *status quo*'.[5]

Again, there is more than one kind of freedom. There is the wilful freedom of mastery and control, the exercise of power in countering opposing power. But there is also the receptive and responsive freedom of recognition and commitment in the face of that which reveals a patient and persuasive authority. Writing in another context, Michael Polanyi well expressed this aspect of both morality and art: 'The freedom of the subjective person to do as he pleases is overruled by the freedom of the responsible person to act as he must'.[6]

Art and morality both belong to the world of freedom, community and the spirit rather than to the world of nature, manipulation and coercion. The world of spirit is an open and unbounded world of shared fundamental values underlying and sustaining a variety of points of view, interpretations and responses. It is a world of community and freedom-in-belonging, in which persons and objects are given the regard due to them. It is a world of communication, in which participants are invited and challenged to share the artist's vision and so to experience at one remove something of the artist's own creativity. The painter Bridget Riley describes this world clearly and succinctly:

> 'Somebody who practises as an artist makes a work but he does not make a work of art. This is done by others: a two-way act is needed. A sort of alchemy turns matter into spirit, and the arena for this transformation is provided by exposure. Unless the work is "seen" in the fullest sense of the word it is obliged to remain a physical object, a personal document or perhaps an idiosyncratic preoccupation. Nobody can truthfully claim it, because each work has to find for itself those who respond to it, those who see it, and those who belong to it.'[7]

Artistic skills can be used for non-artistic and manipulative ends, just as freedom of will can be used for immoral and destructive ends. But when these skills are allied to an artistic integrity which recognises the constraints within which they must work and the ends to which they should aspire, then art and morality may be said to share, each in its own way, a common goal, namely, the enhancement of an authentic and truthful humanity.

Art can take us out of ourselves and reveal to us what is other than ourselves. It can challenge our ordinary ways of perception, in which the unique particularity of an object is reduced to an instance of a general and manageable class of objects. It can teach us that there are more ways than one of 'seeing' the world. It can give us a regard for the self-existence of persons and things no matter their potential utility. It can open our ears to

> That singular command
> I do not understand,
> *Bless what there is for being,*
> Which has to be obeyed, for
> What else am I made for,
> Agreeing or disagreeing?[8]

When the Ancient Mariner saw the 'slimy' waters-snakes as 'blue, glossy green, and velvet black', their every track 'a flash of golden fire', a 'spring of love gushed from [his] heart' and 'blessed them unaware'. So seeing, he was set free from his burden of guilt and fear.[9]

> Mere subjectivity – what I like or dislike, happen to believe or not to believe, and what I propose to make you like, dislike, believe or not believe – is alien to the world of art. One can recognise, and even appreciate, the authenticity of a work of art without necessarily liking it. But Subjectivity, the specifically human capacity to recognise, appreciate and respond, is the lifeblood of art as it is of morality. The Subject is not the maker of values: the Subject is the instrument of evaluation. And true discernment and valid judgement arise out of a disciplined and transformed awareness.

Fear of subjectivity may turn the artist away from the visible world in search of pure form. It may also make him suspicious of introducing any convictional content into his art. But the roots of art in the material world and the human response to that world are not to be forgotten. A convictionless world would be an inhuman world.

Here a distinction between 'direct' and 'indirect' communication is helpful. The poet W H Auden admitted to a strong desire in himself to moralise; at the same time he looked upon any attempt to communicate moral truth directly as an insidious example of the will to exercise power over others. 'You cannot tell people what to do', he wrote, 'you can only tell them parables, and that is what art really is, particular stories of particular people and experiences, from which each according to his immediate and peculiar needs may draw his conclusions'. Convictional art can communicate a vision and yet maintain the reserve and courtesies of a conversation. The artist is a pilgrim rather than a crusader.

A final reflection. We have been following Iris Murdoch in her interpretation of the process of art as a transformation of the self-occupied consciousness into an awareness and appreciation of the beauty of self-existent being. This process nourishes and is nourished by the intellectual and moral virtues of truthfulness, humility and compassion. These virtues, we suggest, are the face of love, for it is of the nature of love to recognise and rejoice in the being of what is other than itself. 'All art, all creativity', the painter David Hockney once said, 'comes from love'.[10] But is not this love gift rather than possession, grace rather than achievement? If so, may we not perhaps proceed to reinterpret the 'pointlessness' of virtue as a reflection of the 'pointlessness' of transcendent Love? Having acknowledged the death of God the controller, are we prepared to experience the resurrection of God the artist? Does art offer us, not only the first steps in morality, but also the first steps in the renewal of love, hope and trust?

Notes

1   Republished in Iris Murdoch, *The Sovereignty of Good*, Routledge & Kegan Paul 1970.

2   Helen Oppenheimer, *The Hope of Happiness*, SCM Press 1983, p. 67.

3   Quoted in Richard Harries, *Art and the Beauty of God*, Mowbray 1993, p. 111.

4   Mary Warnock, *Imagination*, Faber & Faber 1976, p. 207.

5   Quoted in Edward Robinson, *The Language of Mystery*, SCM Press 1987, p. 102.

6   Michael Polanyi, *Personal Knowledge*, Routledge & Kegan Paul 1958, p. 309.

7   Quoted in Edward Robinson, *op.cit.* ,p. 36.

8   W H Auden, *Precious Five*, from "Collected Poems", ed. Edward Mendelson, Faber & Faber 1976.

9   Samuel Taylor Coleridge, *The Rime of the Ancient Mariner*. This observation I have borrowed from Helen Oppenheimer, *op.cit.* She adds: 'The horror departs: not by his choice but by his renewed perception'.

10   Quoted in Richard Harries, *op.cit.*, p. 106. See also "Artists' Statements" in Peter Clothier, *David Hockney*, Abbeville Press 1995, pp. 103-107.

THE LAST JUDGEMENT IN WESTERN ART
PHILIP RYLANDS

THE conviction that good deeds will be rewarded and sins punished by a just God in a life after death, and that a General Resurrection will re-unite the body with the soul, to be granted eternal bliss in Paradise or condemned in perpetuity to frightful suffering, was one of the governing ideas of the Middle Ages. It was shared, *mutatis mutandum*, by Christians and Jews.* This epoch was the heyday of the Last Judgement in art; as Johan Huizinga, in his classic, *The Waning of the Middle Ages* (1931), wrote: "No other epoch has laid so much stress as the expiring Middle Ages on the thought of death". He refers to the "extreme excitability of the medieval soul.... So violent and motley was life, that it bore the mixed smell of blood and of roses. The men of that time always oscillate between the fear of hell and the most naive joy, between cruelty and tenderness, between harsh asceticism and insane attachments to the delights of this world, between hatred and goodness, always running to extremes."

The grip of the Last Judgement on popular imagination in the Middle Ages is vivid all over England where church walls are decorated with Last Judgements known as Dooms. The earliest record of such things, and perhaps their origin, is the Venerable Bede's account of Benedict Biscop, Abbot of Wearmouth, who returning from his fifth journey to Rome around 680 brought with him pictures to decorate his church of St Peter. These included scenes from the Apocalypse of St John, which he placed on the north wall. Typically the Doom decorated the entrance wall or more often the chancel arch where it confronted all who wished to pass from the nave to the altar end of the church, from a state of sin to a state of grace.[1] In 1883 C.E. Keyser listed 109 Dooms in English churches – and these were merely those that had survived the English Reformation.

"Macabre visions as a means of moral exhortation" (another phrase of Huizinga's) is one way of describing perhaps the most famous of English Dooms, in the Church of St Peter and St Paul in Chaldon, Surrey (plate 1), painted c. 1200. This is not strictly speaking a Last Judgement, but it includes many elements that belong to that tradition. With pale figures emerging from a red ochre ground, the cruciform composition is set up by a transverse band of clouds and the vertical Ladder of Salvation (plate 2).[2] The artist draws on a sophisticated Mediterranean tradition for distinguishing between the bestial Demons, their limbs jointed like those of teddy bears and culminating in hoofs or claws, and the placid Angels in togas, their feet elegantly placed at half past three or half past nine, with wings flowing like scarves from their necks. One of the demons stares at us with his tongue stuck out, like the running Gorgon from the archaic Greek pediment of Corfù.

The narrative refers as much to apocryphal texts as to the Bible. In the upper right quadrant, Christ transfixes the devil with his cross-staff in gaping jaws, the Leviathan of which Job speaks (chapter 41). This shark-toothed monster represents the mouth of Hell and of the kingdom of Hades. The scene is the Harrowing of Hell, the redemption of the souls of the Old Testament dead, in the immediate aftermath of the Crucifixion.

It is only alluded to in the Bible – for example: "…Death is swallowed up in victory. O death, where is thy sting? O grave, where is thy victory?" (I Corinthians chapter 15, 54-5). But the full story is told in the Apocryphal Gospel of Nicodemus. The Devil exhorts Hades to make the dead Christ his prisoner, but Christ in Glory triumphs, smashes the Gates of Hell and instead hands the Devil in bondage to Hades. Christ takes the redeemed souls – "the patriarchs and prophets and martyrs and forefathers" – to Paradise, where they are met by Michael the Archangel. The little figure whom Christ holds by the hand in the Chaldon Doom is Adam. Nicodemus also refers to the tree of knowledge and the tree of the cross, depicted in the lower right quadrant. The two small souls that climb the ladder from half way up are Enoch and Elijah the Tishbite, whom God had saved by special dispensation from Death and whom Adam meets on his return to Paradise.

The upper left quadrant represents the Three Maries led to Paradise, while a flying angel delivers the soul of the Good Thief in fulfilment of Christ's promise on the Cross. St Michael, holding a balance, contends with a Devil for the souls of men. His characterisation as a weigher of souls derives from Greek and Egyptian mythology: Mercury weighed the souls of the Heroes on their way to the underworld, while in the elaborate Egyptian ceremony of the Psychostasia, Osiris is the Judge, Maat plays the role of St Michael, and Amemait 'the Devourer' – a hybrid monster, part lion, part hippopotamus, part crocodile – crouches nearby, waiting to devour the hearts of the guilty. An 8th century Cappadocian fresco in Yilanli Kilise shows an angel for the first time with a pair of scales in a Last Judgement context.

The lower level of the Chaldon Doom depicts a place of suffering: Hell, or at best Purgatory. The notion of the fiery furnace is in the Gospel of St Matthew: "So shall it be at the end of the world: the angels shall come forth, and sever the wicked from among the just, And shall cast them into the furnace of fire: there shall be wailing and gnashing of teeth" (chapter 13, 49-50). Tussles, tortures, and squalid encounters illustrate the seven deadly sins, while on the ladder there is more falling than climbing. Unique in its form, but characteristic in its intent, is the element of daily life represented by a saw-like bridge held by two demons, upon which artisans futilely attempt their crafts without the means to do so: the potter has no wheel, the spinner no distaff and the blacksmith no anvil.

The earliest representations of the final reckoning rely on the mystic symbolism of the Revelation or Apocalypse of St John on Patmos. Prudentius, who died in the early 5th century, wrote in his *Dittochaeum* a description in verse of a Roman Basilica with twenty-four Elders (chapter 4, 4), the Slaughtered Lambs and the Book with Seven Seals (chapter 5, 1-9). Pope Leo I (elected in 440) placed Christ with the Four Apocalyptic Beasts (the Tetramorph), and the twenty-four Elders on the façade of St Peter's and in the apse of St Paul Outside the Walls, in Rome. The latter, the four winged

creatures in attendance upon God that both Ezekiel (chapter 1, 4-14) and St John (Revelation chapter 4, 6-8) saw in their visions and which were taken to represent the four Gospel writers Matthew, Mark, Luke and John, appear in the mosaic vault of Galla Placidia's tomb in Ravenna (mid 5th century).[3]

The Gunhild Ivory Cross, c. 1075, was made for the daughter of King Cnut (Gunhild) by a certain Liutger (plate 4). Tiny images in the four extremities and the intersection combine timeless symbolism with more earthy morality: Christ, on the central boss, is surrounded by four archangels and displays the wounds of the Cross. He holds a book inscribed with Alpha and Omega, Christ's pronouncement on three separate occasions in the Revelation of St John. On his right, the Blessed aspire to Heaven, their large hands inscribed with simple cuts across the slight convexity of the ivory. The Damned typically are to the left. But the top and bottom relate the parable of Dives and Lazarus, of the rich man and the beggar. Lazarus is comforted in the bosom of Abraham at the top, and Dives suffers in hell at the bottom (as told in St Luke chapter 16, and as referred to in Revelation chapter 3, in which St John is instructed to inveigh against riches to the Laodiceans). Perhaps the first *Last Judgement*, as opposed to an *Apocalypse*, with all the main elements present, is a Carolingian Ivory in the Victoria Albert Museum (plate 3). This was carved in Tours, around 800. Christ in a nimbus, accompanied by trumpet-blowing angels, presides over the resurrection of the Blessed, succoured another angel, on his right with the damnation of sinners, swallowed by a monster, on his left. A beautiful dancing figure of St Michael moves through the centre of the image.

The theme of the Apocalypse and Last Judgement had much to do with the revival of monumental stone sculpture in Europe. Indeed the great church building revival that marks the 11th century may have been fuelled by the sense of deliverance people felt when the first Millennium passed without terminal incident. Ideas and images spread thanks to the pilgrimage routes and through the presence of sister monasteries of the Abbey of Cluny in Burgundy (1089-1131, now destroyed). In the late 11th century, a compact, seated *Christ in Majesty* with the Tetramorph appeared in the ambulatory of St Sernin, Toulouse, on the road to Santiago de Compostela. The west doorway of the third Abbey church of Cluny had a carved tympanum with a similar *Christ in Majesty*, with angels added. This was surely the prototype for an early masterpiece: the tympanum over the south door of the narthex of St Pierre, Moissac, in Languedoc (c. 1115-35, plate 5). The image illustrates Revelation chapters 4 and 5: the enthroned and royal Christ in a nimbus, with the Book with Seven Seals, is worshipped by the four winged beasts (holding their gospels); before him stretches a sea of glass (surely one of the most spectacular, Surreal images in the Bible); around him are seated the twenty-four elders, with "harps, and golden vials full of odours, which are the prayers of the saints". The lean, six-winged Seraphim on either side of Christ come from the Book of Isaiah (chapter 6, 2). The compression of the figures into a shallow space is

plate 5
Christ in Judgement
c. 1115 - 35
Tympanum of the portal of
St Pierre, Moissac

plate 6
Gislebert of Autun
The Last Judgement
c. 1130 - 35
Tympanum of the west portal
of the cathedral of St Lazare,
Autun

combined with a fully sculptural expressionism – the ceaselessly twisting forms sometimes resembling the strenuous curve of the ploughshare.[4]

In contrast to the hieratic majesty of the tympanum, episodes illustrated to the left of the deep porch make vivid the wages of sin: the tale of Dives and Lazarus, and Devils punishing Lust and Avarice below. These judgemental and punitive themes are transferred to the tympanum itself in the portal of St Lazare, Autun, in Burgundy, c. 1130-35 (plate 6). This includes the weighing of souls, trumpeting angels, the resurrection of the flesh (with one detail *à la* Rodin of giant hands plucking a body from the earth), and, most frightful of all, demons conveying souls to the furnace of hell.

As M.R. James has pointed out in *The Apocalypse in Art* (1931), "… the great Last Judgement scenes which figure so largely on the sculptured tympana of church portals, and in fresco and mosaic, are not as a rule based on the Apocalypse, but depend far more on the Gospels and on extra-Biblical traditions …. the angels blowing the last trump, the other angels who bear the instruments of the Passion, the Virgin and St John – Evangelist or Baptist – interceding, the Judge showing his wounds, St Michael weighing souls, St Peter at the Gate of Paradise; none of these constant and familiar features have anything to do with the Apocalypse." Through the 12th and 13th centuries, from Romanesque to Gothic and even the Tuscan proto-Renaissance, sculptured Last Judgements adorned church portals and Baptistries in innumerable European towns and cities: Beaulieu, Conques, Chartres, Paris (St Denis), Laon, Amiens, Bamberg, Pistoia and Pisa. In the Baptistry at Parma, the chief monument of the art of Benedetto Antelami, built between approximately 1196-1216, a *Last Judgement* over the west door combines the themes of Redemption (Christ reveals his wounds and angels carry the instruments of the Crucifixion), Resurrection (angels blow on trumpets), Mercy (the Six works of Mercy are illustrated on the left door jamb) and Judgement (the Parable of the Labourers in the Vineyard is carved on the right jamb).

The Moissac portal was carved perhaps two generations after mosaicists had pieced together an immense *Last Judgement* in the Basilica of Santa Maria Assunta in Torcello (plate 8), an island at the north end of the Venetian lagoon, which itself is roughly contemporary with the Gunhild Cross. It is probably based on a lost prototype in Constantinople, and makes vivid the differences between West and East in the immediate post-Millennial period. (A Byzantine ivory of the *Last Judgement*, in the Victoria and Albert Museum, London, similar to this mosaic, would have been based on the same prototype.) The uppermost band, double the height of those below, presents a huge Christ redeeming the old testament dead, beginning with Adam. Although most of this was restored in the 19th century, the heads of Christ, Adam, Eve, David and Solomon are originals of the 11th century, as is Hades in disarray at Christ's feet. Below, Christ appears again, seated on the double rainbow (Revelation chapter 4, 3), oddly diminutive, as if distant. At his feet, wheels churn a stream of fire that

plate 7
The Last Judgement
11th - 12th century
detail of the Damned in Hell
Santa Maria Assunta Cathedral,
Torcello, Venice

plate 8 [overleaf]
The Last Judgement
11th - 12th century
Santa Maria Assunta Cathedral,
Torcello, Venice

fuels the flames in Hell, recalling the prophecy of Daniel (chapter 7, 9-10).[5] The Apostles and legions of other saints (not the twenty four Elders), sit on thrones, judging the twelve tribes of Israel, exactly as predicted in St Luke's Gospel (chapter 22, 30). Below them from left to right, the Resurrected rise from the earth (with a docile menagerie of wild animals, including a griffin and an elephant, coughing up their victims), followed by Adam and Eve kneeling before the prepared throne with its sealed book and instruments of the Crucifixion. An Angel with a star spangled scroll recalls St John's terrifying "and the heaven departed as a scroll when it is rolled together" (chapter 6, 14). His draperies and those of the other angels who awake the dead are the most sculptural, lively and sheerly pleasurable designs in the entire mosaic. Their bodies, twisted through almost 180°, are, after all, closely related to the Moissac portal reliefs. Below them the excitement begins. St Michael wars with two demons for the souls of the dead.[6] The river of fire reaches its destination. Two angels, blushing red in the heat, drive the Proud into Hell where the Devil, with the Anti-Christ on his lap, presides. Six other Deadly Sins are boxed in below: the Lustful burn in flames, the Greedy eat their own flesh, the Irate are tossed by the waves, the Envious are consumed by snakes, the Avaricious drown in fire, and the bones of the Idle are strewn about (plates 7). Opposite, St Peter, the Good Thief, the Virgin Mary and Lazarus in the Bosom of Abraham serenely occupy Paradise.

In Padua, not far from Venice, is Giotto's magnificent fresco on the west wall of the Arena Chapel (plates 9 & 10). Like the Torcello mosaic, the *Last Judgement* is only the final episode in a longer story: that of the Incarnation of Christ and the Redemption of the Soul. But Giotto is less interested in the revelation of mystery than in the quandary of mankind. The Cross held aloft by two Angels seems more the proffered means of salvation than the symbol of Christ's sacrifice. With his open right palm Christ welcomes the Elect, but with his left hand turned away he rejects the Damned, who are swept into hell by the river of fire. This compelling detail of the hand that rejects can also be seen in the vault of the Florentine Baptistry, where a 13th-century mosaic *Last Judgement* covers three facets of the octagon. Giotto's hell, like that of the Baptistry, has a monstrous bloated Satan calmly seated while all around suffer reptilian torments. It is the visualisation of the horrors described in rambling apocryphal texts such as the *Book of Enoch*, the *Apocalypse of St Peter*, or more directly, Dante's *Divine Comedy*.[7] Nevertheless a benign atmosphere is also present. The Blessed gently float upwards, as does the praying *Allegory of Hope* on the dado nearby. The Virgin Mary, like an actress in repertoire, appears three different times: stepping down to intercede for the Blessed, and standing (twice) behind the model of the chapel offered by the kneeling donor. The explanation for this is that the previous consecration of the church to the Annunciate Virgin had been overlaid by a new dedication to St Mary of Charity (forgiveness). One Apocalyptic detail: at the top of the fresco flanking the window, two angels in

151

152

plate 9 [previous page]
Giotto di Bondone (c. 1266 -1337)
The Last Judgement
c. 1305
Scrovegni (Arena) Chapel, Padua

plate 10
Giotto di Bondone (c. 1266 -1337)
detail of *The Last Judgement*
c. 1305
Scrovegni (Arena) Chapel, Padua

Byzantine costume peel away the plaster like the burr from an engraver's burin, revealing the gilded but fortified doors of paradise. With this Giotto alludes to 'heaven departing as a scroll'.

The inventory of different punishments meted out for different sins, with monkeyish demons scampering in dark places, has formed our imagination of Hell ever since Giotto's time. St Matthew's account of the second coming (chapter 25, 31-36) offers little more than 'everlasting fire, wailing and gnashing of teeth'. We may not have read Dante's *Divine Comedy* or the *Apocalypse of St Peter*, but we have in our mind's eye such paintings as *The Triumph of Death* and the *Inferno* in the Camposanto of Pisa (painted while the ghastly sights of the Black Death were still fresh in the artist's mind).

The image of Hell in the Duke of Berry's *Trés Riches Heures* (1416, Chantilly, Musée Condé) depicts a gridiron over a furnace, heated with huge bellows. Damned souls fall from the sky and are roasted on the gridiron. A supine, anthropomorphic Satan throws them off; they are renewed and thrust back on, so that they roast once more, *ad infinitum*. The scene is from *Tondale's Book of Visions*, the account of an Irish monk's voyage to hell, which was a precursor of the *Divine Comedy*. Soon after this Jan van Eyck's *Last Judgement* establishes the tradition in the Low Countries for appallingly realistic scenes of the end of the world (plate 11). The hieratic symmetry of Christ, the angels, the Virgin and St John, and the tidy ranks of all the saints (derived from Augustine's *City of God*) contrast with the chaos of hell below. The shallow space of the lower half is crammed with writhing bodies and carnivorous monsters; above Christ reigns over vast and distant panoramas. A narrow strip of flat land- and seascape, with tiny persons resurrecting, divides the two. The use of purely formal means to express opposite conditions of the soul could hardly be bettered, and miraculously all this takes place in a panel a little over a foot in height. The juncture of the elegant St Michael (upright) and the spectral skeleton of Death (horizontal), 'looking' straight out at us, the damned pouring from its groin, ranks with Dürer's *Four Horsemen* as a defining image of Apocalypse.

Rogier van der Weyden painted the enormous *Last Judgement Altarpiece* in nine panels now in the Musée de l'Hôtel-Dieu, Beaune around 1444-48. This answers a question all of us have: when St Michael weighs our souls, is the heavier or the lighter soul the sinner? In Rogier's painting the balance is depressed on the left, where reluctant souls stumble into the valley of death. Opposite, on the side where the scale pan soars, the Blessed are escorted to the 'New Jerusalem' through an ornate Gothic portal.

Twenty years later, Dirk Bouts painted the *Paradise of the Symbolic Fountain* and *Hell* for the Town Hall of Louvain, where he was official painter (plates 12 & 13). What is so striking about Bouts's technique is the crystalline light and minutely realistic flora and fauna with which these totally unreal scenes are presented to us. The spellbinding beauty and strangeness of the Angel with his back to us, his red brocade robe perfectly tailored around his Bird of Paradise

155

plate 11
Jan van Eyck (c. 1380 - 1441)
The Last Judgment
Metropolitan Museum, New York

wings, is an original pictorial invention of extraordinary power. Above and beyond, the Gothic Fountain of Eternal Life and the cosmic 'cloud-tunnel' to Heaven in the sky (again from Augustine's *City of God*) are details that will recur in the paintings of Bosch in the next generation (see below). The reptilian and simian monsters, who are clearly getting the upper hand in their brawl with the damned, are painted like illustrations to a zoological manual. The souls tumbling from the sky, like those in the Limbourg Brothers illumination, suggest once more a reading of *Tondale's Book of Visions*.

The evolution of the Last Judgement theme in Flemish art continued with Hans Memlinc's *Last Judgment Triptych* (1473, Danzig, Muzeum Pomorskie), which combined elements of both Jan Van Eyck's and Rogier van der Weyden's paintings. It was commissioned by Angelo di Jacopo Tani, a representative of the Medici family in Bruges, but was waylaid by a Danzig corsair on its way to Florence. It is tantalising to imagine the effect on Italian painting of such a translation of the Flemish tradition.

Meanwhile, Hieronymus Bosch was beginning his career. His vision of folly, sin and hell represents an impetuous break with the tradition of magic realism that had held sway in Flanders since Van Eyck, and is one of the most extreme, eccentric and inexplicable episodes in the history of art.

The table top in the Prado, Madrid, of c. 1475, may be Bosch's earliest work (plate 14). Three concentric circles represent the all-seeing eye of God: "Cave, cave, Deus videt" is written below the three-quarter length figure of Christ, and what God 'sees' are banal episodes of human weakness, the seven deadly sins performed by ordinary folk in everyday places. The Sin of Pride, or Vanity, depicts a woman of the same class in the same sober interior as Vermeer's *Woman with a Balance* (see page 169). A demon thrusts a mirror on front of her. In the four corners, roundels depict Death, the Last Judgement, the Entry of the Blessed into Paradise, and the Entry of the Damned into Hell.

Although Bosch seems to have spent his entire life in provincial Brabant, his paintings found their way into the collection of the connoisseur-prelate Domenico Grimani in Venice only five years after his death in 1516. These four panels, still today in the Doge's Palace, depict the rise of the blessed into Paradise and the damnation of souls in Hell (plates 15 & 16). They are probably wings of a dispersed *Last Judgement* polyptych. Bouts's narrative has been opened up into four separate moments. The approach of the blessed souls to the fountain of eternal life, accompanied by Angels, is followed by their ascent into Heaven, depicted as a cone of light. Amazingly, the latter cosmic object corresponds to first person accounts of recovery from comas, recollections of birth and even near-death experiences.[8] The second pair depict the descent of souls into Hell and the tortures of the damned. Manifold and esoteric though Bosch's sources were, these scenes are particularly close to the popular *Tondale's Book of Visions*, which was published in Bois-le-Duc, where Bosch lived, in 1484. For example the red hot, glowing river (with suffering souls

158

plate 12
Dirk Bouts (c. 1415 - 75)
Paradise of the Symbolic Fountain
Musée des Beaux-Arts, Lille

plate 13
Dirk Bouts (c. 1415 - 75)
Hell
Musée des Beaux-Arts, Lille

and a cat doing the crawl), occurs in Tondale's vision. These are usually dated c. 1500-3 – exactly contemporary therefore with Luca Signorelli's Orvieto frescoes (see below). They are also contemporary with Dürer's famous woodcuts, but these are, after all, marginal to the Last Judgement theme and doggedly illustrate instead the Apocalypse.

It was only thirty years later that Pope Clement VII conceived the idea of having the *Last Judgement* painted by Michelangelo on the altar wall of the Sistine Chapel (plate 17). This was in the year Henry VIII of England rebelled against the Catholic Church and married Anne Boleyn (1533). But Clement died suddenly in 1534 and it was Pope Paul III who saw the fresco to completion (1534-41). He was determined to have a major work by Michelangelo, and was to be Michelangelo's greatest patron. Paul's reign (1534-49) was the crucible of the Counter Reformation – the founding of the Jesuit Order in 1540 and the first session of the Council of Trent were key events. So this *Last Judgement* was driven both by purely artistic ambition – patronage and connoisseurship – and by a new climate of religious oppression and orthodoxy. It counts as Michelangelo's single greatest work, but also as the most awe-inspiring visualisation of the scene in the history of art. Seething muscular angelic or male bodies are crowded into a shallow space the full height of the wall. The higher the bodies, the larger they get, thus thwarting a sense of distance even in terms of height. Several of the male figures have an unprecedented thickness in the waist – not fat but muscle. Christ has the stature of a man the Italians would call an *armadio*, a cupboard. He raises his right arm and draws his left across his body. The ambiguity of these gestures perfectly expresses the double forces of art and religion bursting asunder in this painting: the right arm, in earlier paintings by Fra Angelico for example, would be raised to welcome the Blessed, while the left arm would point to the spear wound in Christ's side. But in fact the arms function within a mechanism of *disegno*, contrasting rhythmically in their movements exactly as the legs do, in order to create a purely artistic effect of *contrapposto*. Their gestures are virtually deprived of meaning, except an artistic one: virtually, because it is the grace and athleticism of Christ's forward-moving stance that manifests his authority over the whole fresco – despite the fact that Peter and Paul flanking him are larger in size. Nevertheless the febrile virtuosity of Mannerism has begun to take over.

In the lower part of the fresco, there are two distinctly Tuscan elements. To the left, the Resurrection of the Flesh, with bodies, some still skeletal, sluggishly rising from a shelf-like landscape comes from Luca Signorelli's frescoes in Orvieto. Signorelli had been one of the artists who worked on the Moses frescoes on the lower walls of the Sistine chapel. Michelangelo knew him – had even lent him money. Between 1500 and 1503 Signorelli painted *The End of Mankind* in the Cappella Nuova of the Cathedral of Orvieto. This rather complete cycle of frescoes series included *The Antichrist* (with specific reference to Girolamo Savonarola), *The Elect*, *The Last Judgement*, *The Damned* (plate 18)

and *The Resurrection of the Flesh* (plate 19). There is a natural frisson in spying on the dead as they extract themselves from the bare earth, without seriously disturbing the soil, some still 'unclothed' in flesh. Ezekiel's valley of bones is the best Biblical evocation of this scene (chapter 37, 1-14). The Resurrected stand about, as if passing the time of day, in contrast to the torments of the Damned to their left, where sinewy demons, coloured green, purple and grey, with Pan-like faces, riotously 'bother' the miserable sinners. Signorelli's obsession with the nude figure in movement, drawn in all sorts of postures and from all different points of view, makes him Michelangelo's precursor not simply in specific details but generally in his artistic priorities.

Secondly, Michelangelo introduced elements from Dante. The compelling image of Charon, "wild demoniac, with eyes of fire", comes from the third canto of Dante's *Inferno* – an insane figure silhouetted against the horizon, swinging his oar to drive the damned souls into Hades. Minos, Judge of Hades, in the lower right corner, "his tail circled round his body", is another quotation from Dante (*Inferno*, canto 5). Paul III, when the fresco was unveiled, fell to his knees and adroitly phrased the sentiment that every Last Judgement has always provoked: "Lord, charge me not with my sins when thou shalt come on the Day of Judgement".

The Sistine Chapel *Last Judgement* cast its spell over every narrative illustration of the subject henceforth. Tintoretto's enormous canvas (almost six metres in height), which together with its pendant *The Making of the Golden Calf* hangs in the Venetian church of the Madonna dell'Orto, is a case in point (plate 20). It is contemporary with another outsize Venetian painting, Paolo Veronese's *Marriage Feast of Cana* (Paris, Musée du Louvre), and is probably driven by Tintoretto's acute sense of rivalry. It is hard to imagine the Abbot of the monastery proposing something on this scale. He was surely submitting to pressure from the artist. Most obviously however this is Tintoretto's response (or homage) to Michelangelo, who died about the time it was being painted, in 1564.[9] Its commission coincided with another pertinent event: the translation in 1563 of the body of the Venetian reformer Cardinal Gasparo Contarini to the family chapel inside the Madonna dell'Orto. Tintoretto's paintings had a specifically Counter-Reformationary significance and indeed their location in the presbytery of the church negated the age-old role of the *Last Judgement* as an admonition to a frail and sinful congregation – only the monks could see it.

Tintoretto knew Michelangelo's Sistine fresco from prints. From the floodwaters (very Venetian), the Blessed surge upwards and the Damned are swept towards Charon's ferry in the lower right. A silhouetted death's head in the lower part counterpoints the high diminutive figure of Christ the Judge, with Lily and Sword, a detail (though the only one) surely required by the Abbot's attentive reading of St John's Revelation. In between, a cartwheeling angel is the pivot for the vortices of swarming figures. Compared to Michelangelo, there is an interesting reversal. In the lowest

plate 21
Jan Vermeer (1632 - 75)
Woman Holding a Balance
c. 1664
National Gallery of Art,
Washington DC

part of Michelangelo's fresco the light comes from behind the figures, casting an ominous twilight over the barren landscape. The opposite is true in Tintoretto's canvas. The radiant light that shines from behind the flying figures throughout the upper half expresses the Joy of Paradise. The virtuousity in the treatment of color and light that this device required is typically Venetian and is a premonition of the Baroque and Rococo. The potency of each melancholy or vehement, barrel-chested, Herculean figure in Michelangelo's work is replaced in Tintoretto's painting by swathes of athletic figures in ceaseless movement, and by plunging depths of space.

Vermeer's masterpiece of the 1660s, *Woman Holding a Balance* (plate 21), comes at the end of a millennial tradition of depicting the Last Judgement, whether in sculptural relief or in paint. Some of its enduring elements survive here, though translated into the parlour: a scene from daily life (as the context for sin, especially the seven deadly ones), avarice, light and dark charged with metaphor, the scales of St Michael.

The precise meaning of Vermeer's painting, with its *Last Judgement* hung on the wall, has not been defined and perhaps never will be. Its accumulation of familiar symbols and allusions adds up to a conundrum. The woman holds a pair of scales, which she has removed from their box in readiness to weigh, presumably, gold coins or pearls that lie on the table. She holds the scales at the exact centre of the painting, where they are poised in perfect equilibrium. If she were to look up, she would see herself in a mirror. Her head intrudes into the painting of the *Last Judgement* on the wall beyond where she relates, optically at least, to the nimbus of light around Christ, and occupies the place where St Michael, weighing the resurrected souls, would traditionally stand in earlier Flemish painting. In front of her, the virtuous are blessed with eternal life; behind her the sinners are damned to Hell.

The painting on the back wall has not been identified, though its style is that of the Antwerp painter Jacob de Backer, one of the Flemish mannerists of the 16th century among whom the Last Judgement was a popular vehicle for virtuoso nude figure drawing. Examples exist by among others Lucas van Leyden, Jan Prevost, Frans Francken II, Frans Floris, Joos van Cleve and Hendrik Goltzius (plates 22 & 23). Yet from the mid-17th century *Last Judgements* are extremely rare. Rubens's *Large Last Judgement* for the Hofkirche in Neuberg (plate 24), and his two paintings of *The Fall of the Damned* and *The Assumption of the Blessed* of 1621 (both Munich, Alte Pinakothek) are among the last monumental paintings of their kind by a top ranking artist. Appropriately they combine the Italian and Flemish traditions. Tiepolo made a sketch for an oval ceiling of this subject, but seems never to have carried it out. From the 19th century the *Last Judgement* loses altogether its canonical, moral and populist character – vestiges survive only in visionary Romantic painting or subsequently in the 20th-century avant-garde, by which time its specifically Biblical, prophetic and Christian character is gone.

169

170

plate 22
Hendrik Goltzius (1558 - 1617)
The Resurrection of the Dead
British Museum

plate 23
Hendrik Goltzius (1558 - 1617)
The Damned consigned to Hell
British Museum

plate 24
Peter Paul Rubens (1577 - 1640)
The (Large) Last Judgement
1614/16
Alte Pinakothek, Munich

172

The advent of the Age of Reason was accompanied by scepticism regarding religious mysteries. "*Sapere aude*! Have courage to use your own reason – that is the motto of the enlightenment" (Immanuel Kant). It is tempting therefore to attribute the demise of the traditional *Last Judgement* to the Enlightenment. It re-emerges in a sporadic and barely recognisable form in the Romantic period. William Blake was working on a *Last Judgement* over seven feet high at the time of his death in 1827. It was "as black as your hat", according to his friends George and Sidney Cumberland. Earlier drawings by Blake that have survived, such as that in Pollock House, Glasgow, suggest that this would have been in his watery Michelangelo manner. Goya's 'Black Paintings' and his etchings of the *Disasters of War* and *Disparates* re-channel into a modern, secular idiom the veins of horror, fear and cruelty that had driven illustrations of Hell in *Last Judgements* of the by-now distant past. The same was true of Gros's *Napoleon at Eylau* (1808), or Géricault's *Raft of the 'Medusa'* (1819), or Delacroix's *Death of Sardanapalus* (1828).

In 1861 Gustave Doré illustrated Dante's *Inferno*. But perhaps the greatest, the most sublime mid-century representations of the end of the world were those of John Martin, known as 'Mad Martin', who painted a trilogy of the Last Judgement in his last years: *The Great Day of His Wrath* (1851-53, plate 28), *The Last Judgement* and *The Plains of Heaven*, each of them over ten feet wide (all now in the Tate Gallery, London).

The Apocalypse was a perfect vehicle for Martin's Romantic imagination. The title *The Great Day of His Wrath* is taken from the last verse of Revelation chapter 6: "For the great day of his wrath is come: and who shall be able to stand." We are a long way from Giotto's conceit in the Scrovegni Chapel when we see how Martin deals with this text: "And I beheld when he had opened the sixth seal, and lo there was a great earthquake; and the sun became black as sackcloth of hair, and the moon as blood; And the stars of heaven fell unto the earth, … And the heaven departed as a scroll when it is rolled together; and every mountain and island were moved out of their place." The diminutive figures, echoing Michelangelo and the Laocoon, cry "Fall on us and hide us from the face of him that sitteth on the throne, and from the wrath of the lamb." The painting is technically brilliant and magnificent in its 'special effects'.

The late 19th century seems largely to ignore the Last Judgement (as it did John Martin, alas). The figure of Death astride a bat-winged serpent in Arnold Böcklin's *The Plague* (1898, Basle, Öffentliche Kunstsammlung) distantly recalls the skeleton in Van Eyck's *Last Judgement* (plate 11), but his six versions of the *Island of the Dead* are stripped of any Christian vision of the afterlife or of the Resurrection. Jan Toorop's *O Grave Where Is Thy Victory* (1892, Amsterdam, Rijksmuseum) perhaps unwittingly refers to one of the Biblical texts for the Harrowing of Hell. The only major Symbolist contribution to the iconography of the Last Judgement is Rodin's *Gates of Hell* (1880-1917, plate 25). They were never completed and were cast posthumously, in 1926, in their unresolved state

at the end of Rodin's life. Rodin's source is no longer so much the Bible as Dante, with an admixture of Baudelaire. The moody Symbolist tone is set by the Three Shades at the top, who were intended to carry a scroll with the Dantesque invocation "All Hope abandon ye who enter here". Below them, on the lintel, the Thinker is patently derived from a spectral figure on Michelangelo's Sistine fresco. The vague identity of this (Dante? The Repentant Sinner? Mankind? Rodin himself?) and many other figures that teem across all the surfaces make it clear how little force remained in the Last Judgement themes, even those as vivid to the imagination as the Damned in Hell. Indeed the priority given to the artist's creative, expressionist treatment of the nude human figure, as opposed to a set iconographic programme, gives plausibility to an otherwise unlikely theory: that Rodin's 'hellish' mood at the time he began was dispelled when he fell in love with Camille Claudel, and that this was one reason for his failure to complete the work. It may also explain a purely erotic vein: Paolo and Francesca, from canto 5 of the *Inferno,* are perhaps the most famous for this.

175

The Apocalypse was the subject of visionary paintings among the Blue Rider artists immediately before the Great War. Between 1911 and 1913, eschatology dominates Kandinsky's work, with titles such as *All Saints, The Last Judgement, Resurrection*, and *Deluge*. He adopted the notion of Moscow as the New Jerusalem of St John's Vision, as well as of Moscow as the Third Rome (in succession to Constantinople) and the Eternal Capital of Christianity according to Russian Orthodox tradition. This stemmed in the 16th century from a visionary letter from Filofeii of Pskov to the then Grand Prince, and led in turn to Ivan the Terrible's assumption of the title Czar (Caesar). Since the Third Rome was specifically to be the venue for the Third Revelation, that of the Holy Spirit, the title of Kandinsky's famous essay *Über das Geistige in der Kunst* (1911, translated into English in 1914 as *Concerning the Spiritual in Art*) links his theory of art to his millennial and mystic hopes for the spiritual regeneration of Moscow, and of the World. The fashionable Theosophy of Rudolf Steiner and Annie Besant, romantic Neo-Joachism (the revival of Joachim of Fiore's eschatological prophesies around 1200), and the writings of the mystic and Symbolist Dmitrii Merezhkovsky, all contributed to a fever of Millennialism in the early 1900s in Moscow. Thus in Kandinsky's *Small Pleasures* (plate 26), the Kremlin, symbol of Moscow, is identifiable on top of a hill, the Holy Mountain, with three Horseman of the Apocalypse like wire figures by Calder riding back to Heaven (only the Pale Horse is omitted). Again, the vestige of a trumpet blasting angel appears in the top right-hand corner of *Painting with White Border (Moscow)* (1913, New York, Solomon R. Guggenheim Museum), while St George fights the Dragon: St George represents both Muscovite heraldry and the universal struggle of Good against Evil.

In the same circle of the Blue Rider, Franz Marc's devotion to animals was predicated on the belief that man, in a decadent world, needed to re-establish

plate 28
John Martin (1789 - 1854)
The Great Day of His Wrath
1851-53
Tate Gallery, London

plate 29
Paul Nash (1889 - 1946)
Totes Meer (Dead Sea)
1940-41
Tate Gallery, London

the kind of harmonious contact with nature that the animal kingdom enjoyed. His *Fate of the Animals* (1913, plate 27) expresses the conviction that this would come about only through a cataclysmic but healing apocalypse. This masterpiece enlisted the technical innovations of the pre-war avantgardes – Analytical Cubism, Orphism, Rayonnism and Futurism – in the service of a private iconography that drew on such sources as Wagner's *Twilight of the Gods* or Jakob von Hoddis's poem *The End of the World* (1911). Marc's original title was *The Trees Show Their Rings, The Animals Their Veins, and all being is flaming suffering*; its present title we owe to Paul Klee, who restored the lower right-hand corner of the painting after a fire in November 1916, only a few months after Marc had died in Verdun. Marc himself recognised *Fate of the Animals* as a premonition of the horrors of the Great War battlefields. In 1913-14, he painted *Tyrol* (Munich, Bayerisches Staatsgemäldesammlungen), in which the radiant presence of a Mother and Child, with the Sun and Moon, is an explicit reference to the Revelation of St John, chapter 12.

The depiction of Hell, the desolate landscape as a setting for suffering and death, has its equivalent in other war paintings in the 20th century. When Paul Nash, the British Neo-Romantic, was assigned to the front at Passchendaele in November 1917, it transformed his until then minor talent. His greatest painting of this kind however belonged to the Second World War, when he was again an official war artist. *Totes Meer (Dead Sea)* (plate 29) depicts a German fighter plane dump in Cowley, Oxford. The buckled and torn metal surges like storm waves beating against the sea barriers of some of Nash's earlier paintings of Dymchurch in Sussex. Cruelty, barbarism and malevolence are expressed in a richly allusive way. The melancholy Samuel Palmer-ish moon and the solitary flight of the owl hint at the diabolic or at some natural calamity (*Totes Meer* is often compared to Caspar David Friedrich's *Arctic Shipwreck* of c. 1823-24, now in Hamburg). The low viewpoint and high horizon menace us, as if there is the risk if drowning. The rent wing of a plane, with a Nazi Military Cross, doubles as a displaced gravestone after the Resurrection.

One of Nash's fellow students at the Slade School in 1910-11 was Sir Stanley Spencer. Spencer painted Resurrection themes at various times throughout his life, beginning with *The Resurrection, Cookham* (1924-26, London, Tate Gallery), set in Cookham churchyard, in Berkshire. This was in his first one-man show in the Goupil Galleries, London. Twenty years later he painted his 'Port Glasgow Resurrection series'- eighteen canvases in all. They were the expression of his feelings of joy when working as an official artist in the Port Glasgow shipyards during the Second World War. The main group consisted of three paintings that Spencer intended to be hung one above the other. At the top, comical pneumatic *Angels of the Apocalypse* (private collection) sail through the sky, fertilising the earth with seeds spilling from Beaufort Hospital bed bottles. At the bottom would have been the long frieze-like *Resurrection, Port Glasgow* (London, Tate Gallery). In between, *The Resurrection: The Hill of Zion* (plate 30)

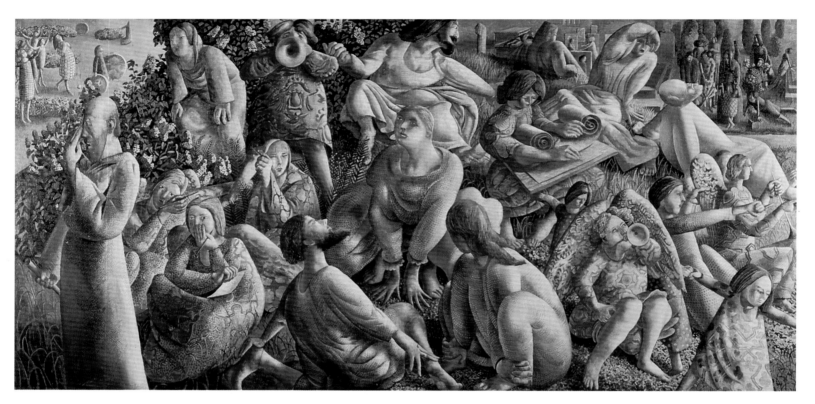

presents Christ seated in a field of lilac issuing apocalyptic commands from a shallow convex hillock in Port Glasgow cemetery. Two angels blow trumpets and a third records mankind's good deeds with the help of a scroll. A prophet on the left surveys the horizon and in the background young souls resurrect or make their way to paradise. Three figures (two disciples and the Virgin Mary?) form a perfect equilateral pyramid at Christ's feet: they may be a literal example of Spencer's own reference to the symbolism of his forms in this painting. But the spontaneous expression of innocent joy is expressed not through conventional symbols (the triangle = the Trinity) so much as by the purely visual elements: the forms, lines, postures, colours and composition. The disciple squatting, with his hands holding his ankles, is perfect. The benign essence of Spencer's peculiarly English art in these paintings, where Hell plays no part and in which the spring sun shines on the last days, is hardly typical of the genre and extraordinary for the most bellicose and bloodthirsty century in the history of man, as it delivers us cheerfully to a non-judgemental conclusion.

179

Notes

* I am grateful to Nicholas de Lange for sharing with me his article on this subject.

1 The late 15th-century *Last Judgement* that wraps around the Chancel Arch of St Thomas's, Salisbury, has been described as "one of the largest, completest and comparatively best preserved" (Albert Hollaender, 1944).

2 Although it has been argued that this is more properly a Purgatorial Ladder (making the lower band of the painting Purgatory itself), because the figures as they ascend and descend are nude not clothed, the notion of Purgatory as the intermediate level between Hell and Heaven does not fully enter the Catholic imagination until the 14th century, in the wake of Dante's *Divine Comedy*.

3 Nevertheless, no carved or painted representation of these four creatures can ever match the fantastical word-pictures given by both Ezekiel and John.

4 The source for the Moissac tympanum has been traced to illuminated manuscripts. This is evident from the pervasive calligraphic line. Specifically, it is based on a copy commissioned by a Spanish Abbot of Saint Sever, Gregory of Montana, of Beatus of Liebana's commentaries on the Apocalypse and the Book of Daniel. A Spanish pre-occupation with eschatological texts may be connected to a hope of release from the Moorish occupancy at the time of the first Millennium.

5 The four apocalyptic beasts peek like naughty pets from behind the wings of the two Seraphim. They are in perpetual attendance on the wheels of the carriage in Ezekiel's vision (chapter 1, 15-21).

6 Irina Andreescu, foremost authority on these mosaics, has identified in this group a late 12th-century restoration by the workshop of the Ascension Master, whose mosaics in the crossing of St Mark's in Venice are among the most dynamic and expressionist in the whole of Middle Byzantine art.

7 Enrico Scrovegni built the chapel and commissioned the frescoes. The presence in Giotto's hell of usurers, hung from their necks by their purse strings, reminds one that Enrico's father, Reginaldo was the Paduan usurer in the 17th canto of the *Inferno*, who "lolled his tongue all wet, As does an ox which sets itself to lick its snout".

8 This was pointed out to me by Tom Pocock.

9 According to Tintoretto's 17th-century biographer, Tintoretto had inscribed on a wall of his studio the slogan "Michelangelo's design and Titian's colour".

CONTRIBUTORS

ANTHONY CARO

Anthony Caro was born in Surrey, England, in 1924. He is a pivotal figure in the development of sculpture in the Twentieth Century. After studying sculpture at the Royal Academy Schools in London he worked as assistant to Henry Moore. Following his early years, when he worked mostly with clay and bronze, he first came to prominence with a show at the Whitechapel Gallery in 1963. There he exhibited large brightly painted abstract sculptures that stood directly on the floor and which engaged the spectator directly on a one-to-one basis. This was a radical departure from the way sculpture had previously been seen. His sculpture is usually made in steel but he also works in a diverse range of materials including bronze, silver, lead, paper, clay, stoneware and wood.

Caro taught for two years at Bennington College, Vermont, USA, and for many years at St Martin's School of Art in London where his students included Philip King, Barry Flanagan, Richard Long, Gilbert & George and Richard Deacon. Both his innovative sculpture and the questioning approach of his teaching opened up many new possibilities both formally with subject matter. This led to a flowering and a new confidence in sculpture worldwide.

He held a one-man retrospective at the Museum of Modern Art, New York, in 1975, *Sculpture into Architecture* at the Tate Gallery in 1991, further retrospectives at the Trajan Markets, Rome, in 1992, and the Museum of Contemporary Art, Tokyo, in 1995, and *Sculpture from Painting* at the National Gallery in London in 1998.

He has been awarded numerous prizes including the Premium Imperiale for Sculpture in Tokyo in 1992 and holds many honorary degrees amongst which are those he received from Yale and Cambridge Universities. He is also an honorary member of the American Academy of Arts & Letters, the American Academy of Arts and Sciences and the Brera Academy in Milan. He was knighted in 1987.

WÜRTH AND THE ARTS

The Würth Group was founded in Künzelsau by Adolf Würth in 1945. When he died suddenly in 1954 his son Reinhold took over its management. Today Würth is a worldwide group which operates in 73 countries with a total of 191 companies and nearly 30,000 employees.

Reinhold Würth has collected art for more than 20 years and the Museum Würth is the result of his commitment to the arts and culture. Since the museum opened in 1991, under the directorship of Sylvia Weber, over 650,000 people have visited its exhibitions which have included *Gaugin and the Pont Aven School*, *Christo* and *Picasso: His Dialogue with Ceramics*.

The Museum Würth has a collection of over 4,500 items including paintings by Picasso, Tapies, German and international figurative painting from the Sixties to the Nineties and the entire graphic work of Max Ernst. The collection also focuses on 20th-century sculpture and includes works by Jacobsen, Chillida, Max Bill and Caro. A new museum, due for completion in 2001, is at present being constructed in Schwäbisch Hall, near Stuttgart.

The Würth Foundation was established in 1978 to promote the arts and sciences. The Foundation awards prizes and funds other initiatives in the field of music, visual arts, literature and performances.

ROBERT HINDE

A distinguished scholar on the subject of animal behaviour, former Master of St John's College, University of Cambridge and a Royal Society Research Professor. He is interested in the links between the biological and social sciences. He has spent a career forging links between studies of animals in their natural settings and animal psychology. In the last decade he has focused on the origins of aggression and war. His publications include *Relationships: a Dialectical Perspective* (1997), *War: some psychological causes and consequences* (1997), and *Why Gods persist: a scientific approach to religion* (1999).

HANS MAGNUS ENZENSBERGER

Widely regarded as one of the greatest living poets of the German language, he is also a writer of prose, drama and cultural criticism. He is a provocative cultural essayist and his poems have included harsh criticism of our post-war society that is based on prosperity and perhaps a false sense of well-being. One of Europe's leading political thinkers, his other important publications include *poems for people who don't read poems* (1968), *The Sinking of the Titanic* (1978), *Civil War* (1994) and *Kiosk* (1997). He has received numerous prizes and honours, including the Georg Brückner Prize, the Premo Pasolini Prize and most recently the Ernst-Robert-Curtis Prize.

NADINE GORDIMER

South African novelist and one of the strongest voices against apartheid over the last 30 years. Her main themes are relationships and behaviour in a split society. She was a founding member of the Congress of South African Writers and her major works include *The Conservationist* (1974), *Burger's Daughter* (1979), (which was banned after the Soweto uprising), *July's People* (1981), *Crimes of Conscience* (1991), and *The House Gun* (1998). She was awarded the Nobel Prize for Literature in 1991.

JOHN SPURLING

Playwright, novelist and critic, his first play, *MacRurie's Guevara* was produced by the National Theatre, London, in 1969. He has written some 25 plays for stage, radio and television. His first novel, *The Ragged End*, was published in 1989 followed by *After Zenda* in 1995. He was the New Stateman's art critic from 1976 to 1988 and continues to contribute occasional art reviews for *The Spectator* and the *Royal Academy Magazine*. To accompany Caro's *Trojan War* at the Yorkshire Sculpture Park in 1994 he wrote the play *Achilles on the Beach at Troy* as well as contributing his own translations from Homer with descriptions of Homer's characters to the exhibition catalogue.

DAVID BUCKLAND

British born artist whose scope encompasses photography, portraiture, set and costume design for the theatre. Solo exhibitions include *Performances* at the National Portrait Gallery 1999, the Musée National d'Art Moderne (Centre Georges Pompidou), the Minneapolis Institute of Art and the Espace Photographique de la Ville de Paris. Theatre designs include the Siobhan Davies Dance Company and the Royal Ballet, London.

PETER BAELZ

A contemporary of Caro's at Christ's College, University of Cambridge, where he received a double first in Classics and Theology and was a double blue. He became Professor of Moral and Pastoral Theology at Oxford University and later was Dean of Durham Cathedral where he instigated an 'Artists in Residence' scheme. His special subject is ethics and the philosophy of religion and his publications include *Does God Answer Prayer?* (1893) and *Ethics and Belief* (1977).

PHILIP RYLANDS

Philip Rylands is an art historian who has lived in Venice since 1973. From 1974-84 he worked with the Venice in Peril Fund, a committee for the saving of Venetian art and architecture, including restoration projects such as the Porta della Carta, San Nicolò dei Mendicoli, the Basilica of Torcello and the Oratorio dei Crociferi. His publications include *Restoring Venice: The Church of the Madonna dell'Orto* (1976, with Sir Ashley Clarke) and *Palma il Vecchio* (1988). He is currently Deputy Director of the Peggy Guggenheim Collection (Solomon R. Guggenheim Foundation) in Venice.

ACKNOWLEDGEMENTS

184 **EDITOR**

Ian Barker

DESIGNER

Kate Stephens

PHOTOGRAPHER

David Buckland

page 52: Tom Wolfe, *The Bonfire of the Vanities,* Jonathan Cape
page 84: Ross Macdonald, *Black Money,* HarperCollins Publishers Ltd
page 110: Isaac Deutscher, *Stalin: A Political Biography,* Andrew Nurnberg Associates
page 76: Samir al-Khalil, *Republic of Fear: Saddam's Iraq* , Hutchinson
page 106: General Sir Michael Rose, Lines from *Fighting for Peace* © The Rose Partnership 1998,
first published in 1998 by The Harvill Press Limited. Reproduced by permision of The Harvill Press Ltd.
page 114: W.H. Auden, *The Shield of Achilles,* Faber and Faber Ltd
page 116: William Empson, *Missing Dates,* Lady Empsom / Hogarth Press
plates 16, 17, 18, 24: AKG London
plate 6: AKG London / Stefan Drechsel
plate 25: AKG London / Erich Lessing
plates 8, 20: Osvaldo Böhm, Venice
plates 1, 2: David Buckland
plates 22, 23: © British Museum
plates 5, 7, 9, 10, 14, 15, 19, 21, 27: Bridgeman Art Library, London / New York
plate 30 : Bridgeman Art Library, London / New York / © Estate of Spencer 1999. All rights reserved DACS
plate 4: The Conway Library, Courtauld Institute of Art
plates 12, 13: Giraudon / Bridgeman Art Library, London / New York
plate 11: The Metropolitan Museum of Art, Fletcher Fund, 1933 (33.92b)
plate 26: Sally Ritts / © The Solomon R. Guggenheim Foundation, New York (FN 43.921)
plates 28, 29: Tate Gallery, London 1999
plate 3: V&A Picture Library

Transport: MTEC Internationel Ltd and Gondrand S.p.A
Plan of the exhibition drawn by Oxford Illustrators and Gavin Morris
Printed by CTD, Twickenham, Middlesex

ISBN 3 934350 00 3
© The authors , Museum Würth and Verlag Paul Swiridoff, Künzelsau